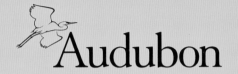
Audubon

BIRDING ADVENTURES

FOR KIDS

For Steve and Liliana Pearl: You are my dawn chorus and the wind beneath my wings.
—**Elissa Wolfson**

To Adam: Your humor, kindnesses, and all-round support carry me on.
—**Margaret A. Barker**

Inspiring | Educating | Creating | Entertaining

Brimming with creative inspiration, how-to projects, and useful information to enrich your everyday life, Quarto Knows is a favorite destination for those pursuing their interests and passions. Visit our site and dig deeper with our books into your area of interest: Quarto Creates, Quarto Cooks, Quarto Homes, Quarto Lives, Quarto Drives, Quarto Explores, Quarto Gifts, or Quarto Kids.

© 2020 Quarto Publishing Group USA Inc.
Range Maps © 2020 Cornell Lab of Ornithology

First Published in 2020 by Cool Springs Press, an imprint of The Quarto Group,
100 Cummings Center, Suite 265-D, Beverly, MA 01915, USA.
T (978) 282-9590 F (978) 283-2742 QuartoKnows.com

Cool Springs Press titles are also available at discount for retail, wholesale, promotional, and bulk purchase. For details, contact the Special Sales Manager by email at specialsales@quarto.com or by mail at The Quarto Group, Attn: Special Sales Manager, 100 Cummings Center, Suite 265-D, Beverly, MA 01915, USA.

23 22 21   3 4 5

ISBN: 978-0-7603-6608-0

Digital edition published in 2020
eISBN: 978-0-7603-6609-7

Library of Congress Cataloging-in-Publication Data available.

Design and Page Layout: Megan Jones Design
Cover Image: Shutterstock, except back left (Maxwell Ramey, Youth Maryland Ornithological Society), and back right (Matthew Addicks, Youth Maryland Ornithological Society)
Range Maps: The Birds of North America, birdsna.org, maintained by the Cornell Lab of Ornithology

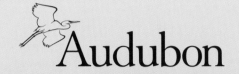

BIRDING
ADVENTURES

ACTIVITIES AND IDEAS
FOR WATCHING, FEEDING,
AND HOUSING OUR
FEATHERED FRIENDS

ELISSA WOLFSON *and* MARGARET A. BARKER

COOL
SPRINGS
PRESS

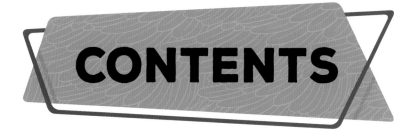

CONTENTS

CHAPTER 1

MEET THE BIRDS:

25 KINDS OF BIRDS
TO SEE, HEAR,
AND LEARN ABOUT 11

CHAPTER 2

OUTSIDE WITH THE BIRDS:

GAMES, ACTIVITIES,
AND ADVENTURES 47

CHAPTER 3

INSIDE WITH THE BIRDS:

GAMES, ACTIVITIES, AND ADVENTURES 69

APPENDIX: LEARN MORE AND GET INVOLVED! 88

↠ The Great Blue Heron has a long, dagger-like bill.

INTRODUCTION

> "Wherever you live, birds live there, too. The first step is to simply pay attention."
> —NOAH STRYCKER, BIRD WRITER/PHOTOGRAPHER

Some people are fascinated with birds, while others barely notice them! Many people's lifelong love of birds started when they were kids. Look where it has taken some of them:

- **ROGER TORY PETERSON** (1908–1996) wrote that his life's work was sparked by a beautiful color picture of a Blue Jay that his seventh grade teacher gave him to copy. After that, birds became an obsession. Roger went on to become a world-famous bird artist and field guide author.

- When she was 11, **CLAIRE WAYNER**'s grandfather gave her a bird guide. Eager to learn more, she joined the Youth Maryland Ornithological Society (YMOS), organized bird festivals, and competed in the World Series of Birding. Now at college, Claire studies environmental engineering and has co-founded a campus bird group.

- **TED GILMAN**'s parents set him on the path to birding. When he was a baby, they put his playpen on the front porch so Ted could see and hear the birds around his home. Today, Ted is a senior naturalist and environmental educator at the Audubon Center in Greenwich. He's taught thousands of children about birds and nature.

- **NOAH STRYCKER** still remembers how his fifth grade teacher in Oregon set up a bird feeder outside a classroom window. The moment a bird landed, she'd stop everything. Students would scramble to identify the feathered visitor from a bird poster on the wall. Since those days, Noah has written three books. *Birding Without Borders* is all about his around-the-world adventure, during which he observed 6,042 different bird species in one year!

Claire Wayner observes breeding birds in the highlands of western Maryland.

A male Eastern Bluebird plops a mealworm into his fledgling's wide-open beak.

Binoculars help kids put their eyes to the skies!

BIRDY CAREERS

Bird-related careers include writing about birds, helping endangered birds, managing bird sanctuaries, teaching people about birds, and rehabilitating injured wild birds. Bird scientists, or ornithologists, study bird songs, feathers, migration, behavior, and more.

Start by creating your own birding adventures with your family and friends. Try watching birds near your home or school, putting up feeders and nest boxes, taking bird walks at parks and nature centers, joining bird clubs, going to bird festivals, or taking a bird-focused family vacation. Your birding adventures may take you in unexpected directions and your memories will last a lifetime!

HOW TO USE THIS BOOK

On the pages that follow, you'll find a guide to dozens of the common birds around you. You can start by reading about and familiarizing yourself with these birds in Chapter 1. Or, get outside and then come back to these profiles to help you identify what you saw or heard. Every profile includes the bird's unique features (field marks) along with its length, voice, feeding habits, the challenges it faces (conservation status), and, most importantly, things you can do to help that bird. Bird profiles also include range maps. These show you where birds can be found at certain times of the year. For example, many U.S. birds spend the summer in Canada and the winter in Mexico.

In Chapter 2, the outside activities chapter, you'll discover bird-walking, binoculars, and bird games. You'll also learn to attract wild birds with food, water, and shelter. Then bring the fun indoors! Chapter 3 contains all sorts of activities for rainy or snowy days at home or in school. Activities include more bird games, bird experiments, and building simple bird homes.

Throughout the book you'll find fun facts and jokes, too. As a group, birders like to laugh and pass along a smile to the next generation (that's you!).

You'll soon discover that birds are everywhere. You just have to see or hear them. You can see bird images in books and on posters. You can watch birds online on live-streaming bird cameras. Birds are in your backyard, in parks, and even in parking lots. Sometimes they're right outside your windows at home or school.

Let's go birding!

In the future, this tiny oak might grow into a home for both birds and the insects they feed on. Planting and protecting trees like native oaks helps create a more bird-friendly world.

BIRD LOVER FOR LIFE: DR. STEPHEN KRESS

Founder of Project Puffin/Vice President
for Bird Conservation, National Audubon Society

I trace my bird interest to my fourth grade teacher in Ohio, who steered me to birds. One spring day, Mrs. Reed spotted a bird below her second-floor classroom window. She gathered the class around and asked, "Who can identify that brown bird pecking at the ground?" I took the challenge head-on and ran to get a Golden Guide (a simple, popular nature guide series) from the classroom shelf. When that robin-size bird flew up, showing its white rump and a flash of yellow underwing, I thumbed through the book to the drawing of a Northern (then called Yellow-shafted) Flicker. It was my first success at bird identification! After that, on many nights, my mom would find me asleep with the light still on and a Golden Guide at my pillow.

Dr. Steve Kress examines an Atlantic Puffin on Eastern Egg Rock. This small island off the coast of Maine is home to the world's first restored Atlantic Puffin colony.

I hope that the readers of this book will become interested in birds, and perhaps even make a career out of watching and helping birds. That's what I did. And I feel fortunate every day to know that I am helping puffins and other seabirds survive the many challenges of our time through Project Puffin, the seabird restoration project I started in 1973.

Birds need more friends! There are many things you can do, even in your own home, backyard, or schoolyard to help local birds. By watching birds and doing activities such as those in this book, you will experience the special spark of seeing birds wherever you go. Your spark will grow if you feed it! Consider a family camp or, for older birders, a teen birding session at the Hog Island Audubon Camp in Maine (hogisland.audubon.org).

This connection between birds, nature, and stewardship is the foundation of the Audubon movement. Clearly, when we take care of birds, we are also taking care of this precious planet that we call home.

1 MEET THE BIRDS:

25 KINDS OF BIRDS TO SEE, HEAR, AND LEARN ABOUT

If you're excited to get outside and start birding, turn right to Chapter 2! Plan on going out at dawn or dusk, when birds are most active. But any time is a good time to go birding. Strap on those binoculars and see what birds live in your neighborhood; then come back to this chapter for help identifying them.

Note: The birds in this chapter are just a tiny fraction of the 1,100-plus bird species in the United States alone. But getting to know them will be a good start to your birding journey!

The birds you'll find on the following pages are all common, meaning there's a good chance you can see many of them where you live. Some can be seen at bird feeders; others are found in specific places, such as bodies of water. When you see a bird you want to know more about, first look around you—that's the bird's habitat. You wouldn't expect to see a Mallard duck in a tree or a woodpecker paddling on a pond! That's because ducks practically live on water, while woodpeckers live in trees. Don't forget to listen as well as look! It's often easier to *hear* a bird song than *see* the bird singing.

These bird profiles are listed alphabetically by the bird's common name. Their scientific names are in italics. The profiles describe the bird's field marks—markings such as colors, spots, and stripes that help you identify it. You'll also find out the bird's length from head to tail, its sound, and what it eats. Conservation status tells you whether it is abundant or becoming rare. But even common birds need help to stay common! So you'll also find out what you can do to help them. Finally, you'll discover some cool, fun facts about each bird.

COMMON BIRD HABITATS

BIRDS IN A CITY: crows, House Sparrows, pigeons, robins, starlings

BIRDS BY A LAKE: ducks, geese, gulls, Red-winged Blackbirds

BIRDS AT FEEDERS: Blue Jays, cardinals, chickadees, finches, hummingbirds, juncos, Mourning Doves, nuthatches, sparrows, Tufted Titmice, woodpeckers

BIRDS IN A FIELD: bluebirds, hawks, Tree Swallows, Turkey Vultures, Wild Turkeys

←← Birdbath party time! Juvenile Eastern Bluebirds splash and play in their own do-it-yourself birdbath—a sundial filled with rainwater.

BLACKBIRD

RED-WINGED BLACKBIRD

(Agelaius phoeniceus)

FIELD MARKS: As you might guess from their name, male Red-wings have bright red shoulder patches. Males are glossy black; females are streaky brown.

LENGTH: 8½" (22 cm)

VOICE: The male's enthusiastic *"Conk-a-ree,"* often sung from a cattail, is a sign of spring!

FEEDING: Flocks gather in fields during migration to feed on seeds and grain. They eat insects during breeding season.

CONSERVATION: Abundant but declining since the 1960s.

HOW YOU CAN HELP: Scatter grain or seeds on the ground where migrating Red-wings prefer to feed. Protect the wetlands and tall grasses where they nest.

DID YOU KNOW? Males flash their brilliant red shoulder patches to impress females and warn away other males. When they are at rest, the red patches are hidden, but the yellow borders may peek out.

Fun Fact:
Winter roosting flocks can contain millions of Red-wings and other species. These flocks disperse each morning to feed and they reconvene each night.

SIMILAR SPECIES: California's Tricolored Blackbirds

Breeding male Red-winged Blackbirds spend lots of time defending their territory.

RANGE MAP FOR RED-WINGED BLACKBIRD

- Breeding
- Nonbreeding
- Year-round

BLUEBIRDS

EASTERN BLUEBIRD

(Sialia sialis)

FIELD MARKS: Males are bright blue, with rusty orange throats and chests, and white bellies. Females have blue-gray backs and pale orange chests. Males may appear gray-brown from farther away. That's because their blue color depends upon the lighting.

LENGTH: 7" (18 cm)

VOICE: A series of soft, whistled notes: "*Chur, chur, chur-ly, chur-ly!*"

FEEDING: Bluebirds eat wild fruits and berries in the winter. In warmer weather, they capture protein-rich insects such as grasshoppers and caterpillars. They can even spot these bugs when perched 150 feet (46 m) away!

CONSERVATION: Bluebirds need open fields and meadows to live. In the 1900s, bluebird populations plummeted—they lost habitat to agriculture and development, and they faced competition from non-native birds. With human help, they have made a great comeback.

Cool!
One Eastern Bluebird's leg band proved it was more than 10 years old. That made it the oldest known of its species!

WHAT BIRD IS SAD?
A "blue" bird

(continued)

This perched male Eastern Bluebird scans the ground for insect prey. He might have his eye on a juicy grasshopper!

RANGE MAP FOR EASTERN BLUEBIRD

Breeding
Winter
Year-round

Male Mountain Bluebird

HOW TO HELP: You can build nest boxes for all three bluebird species. Bluebirds seem to like these just as much as hard-to-find natural tree cavities. A dish of live mealworms might also attract bluebirds to your yard.

SIMILAR SPECIES: Western Bluebirds replace their Eastern cousins in the Western United States. But these males have a blue (not orange) throat. Females are paler than males. Mountain Bluebirds are found in high Western areas. Males are turquoise all over with white bellies. Females are brownish-gray with blue-tinged wings and tails.

Cool!
Bluebirds are often seen as a sign of spring and better times ahead. "The bluebird of happiness" is a common phrase.

BLUEBIRD HERO

In the 1970s, bluebirds became rare. Lawrence Zeleny (a.k.a. "Dr. Z") wrote a book called *The Bluebird: How You Can Help Its Fight for Survival.* Dr. Z founded the North American Bluebird Society. He also designed a starling-proof nest box that helped restore bluebird populations. People have since put up thousands of bluebird boxes. Dr. Z monitored his own nest boxes until he was 91!

A female Eastern Bluebird brings nesting materials to her mate at the nest box. Both parents build the nest, which will hold 2 to 7 pale blue eggs.

Male Western Bluebirds like this one have bright blue throats.

CARDINAL

NORTHERN CARDINAL

(*Cardinalis cardinalis*)

FIELD MARKS: The fire engine red male cardinal is hard to miss! Females are warm brown with red accents. Both have black faces; short, thick red bills; and crests (feathers sticking up on top of the head).

LENGTH: 8½" (22 cm)

VOICE: A loud, clear, whistled "*Cheer, cheer, cheer!*" Both males and females sing.

FEEDING: Cardinals eat seeds, fruit, and sometimes insects. They often visit bird feeders.

What's up? The crest of this female Northern Cardinal, that's what's up!

CONSERVATION: Cardinals were once caught and sold as caged pets. Bird protection laws made that illegal. Their numbers have grown in recent decades, partly because more people have beneficial backyard habitats.

HOW YOU CAN HELP: Brushy undergrowth can attract nesting cardinals to your yard. They also like black oil sunflower seeds. Put some in your feeder!

DID YOU KNOW? The oldest known Northern Cardinal was a female who was almost 16 years old.

The male cardinal's colors make it popular. Seven states list the Northern Cardinal as their state bird!

RANGE MAP FOR NORTHERN CARDINAL

Year-round

Fun Fact:
Chickadees respond to pishing sounds by coming closer. They seem curious about humans.

CHICKADEE

BLACK-CAPPED CHICKADEE

(Poecile atricapillus)

Cool!
These tiny birds survive freezing cold winter nights by huddling in tree cavities. They drop their body temperatures and fluff up their feathers.

FIELD MARKS: Chickadees have black caps, black bibs, and big white cheek patches.

LENGTH: 5½" (14 cm)

VOICE: Chickadees call out their name: "*Chick-a-dee-dee-dee!*" Their song is a clear, whistled "*FEE-bee-bee.*"

FEEDING: Chickadees eat insects, seeds, and berries all day to replace calories lost at night.

CONSERVATION: Abundant throughout their range

HOW YOU CAN HELP: Plant fruits like wild cherries, blackberries, and blueberries. Put up nest boxes. Provide black oil sunflower seeds and suet at feeders.

DID YOU KNOW? Chickadees hide hundreds of seeds daily. They can remember where they hid them a month later!

SIMILAR SPECIES: These include Carolina Chickadees in the Southeast, Mountain Chickadees in the West, and Boreal Chickadees in the north. The Tufted Titmouse (left) is in the same family as chickadees and is a frequent visitor to eastern bird feeders.

Black-capped Chickadee

RANGE MAP FOR BLACK-CAPPED CHICKADEE

Year-round

CROW

AMERICAN CROW

(*Corvus brachyrhynchos*)

FIELD MARKS: American Crows are all black, from beak to tail.

LENGTH: 17½" (45 cm)

VOICE: Series of loud "*caws*"

FEEDING: Nuts, seeds, fruit, insects, shellfish, mice, and the eggs and chicks of other birds

CONSERVATION: Crows are abundant everywhere, including cities. Some people dislike crows for eating crops, or because of the noise and droppings from their large winter roosts. Crows are hunted as pests in many states, though they are usually not eaten.

HOW YOU CAN HELP: Teach others about these bright-eyed, brainy birds, and more people may learn to live with them.

DID YOU KNOW? Crows have strong families. "Teenage" crows help parents care for younger siblings.

WHAT KIND OF CROWS ALWAYS STICK TOGETHER?
Vel-crows!

SIMILAR SPECIES: Fish Crows, found in eastern costal states, have a nasal "*uh-uh*" call. Common Ravens are much larger than crows. They're found mostly in western states and are widespread in Canada and Mexico.

Crows are among the most intelligent and social birds. Their winter roosts can consist of tens of thousands of crows!

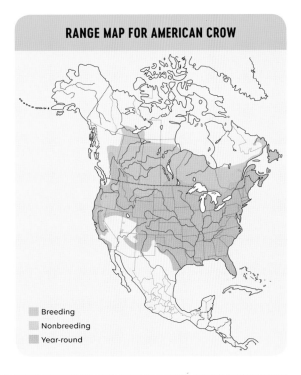

RANGE MAP FOR AMERICAN CROW

Breeding
Nonbreeding
Year-round

MOURNING DOVE

(Zenaida macroura)

FIELD MARKS: Soft brown all over, Mourning Doves have black spots on their back and a buffy belly. The long, pointy tail shows white edges in flight. Males and females look alike.

Fun Fact: Mated pairs nest long before most other species, sometimes when snow still lingers.

Ground-feeding Mourning Doves store seeds in their crops (throat pouches). Then they can eat any time they want!

LENGTH: 12" (31 cm)

VOICE: Named for its mournful *"Hoo-OOO, hooo, hooo"* call, the Mourning Dove is often mistaken for an owl. Its wings make a whistling sound upon take-off.

FEEDING: This fast-flying dove feeds almost entirely on grains and small seeds. Unlike most birds, the Mourning Dove uses its bill like a straw to suck up water.

CONSERVATION: One of the most abundant birds in the U.S., with a population of about 350 million. Mourning Doves are living reminders of the related, now-extinct Passenger Pigeons, which were once so numerous that flocks darkened the sky.

HOW YOU CAN HELP: Provide cracked corn, millet, and sunflower seed in tray feeders. Try giving them milo, too. Most birds don't like it, but these doves do. Install Mourning Dove nesting cones in the forked branches of conifer trees.

DID YOU KNOW? Mourning Doves are found in every state.

RANGE MAP FOR MOURNING DOVE

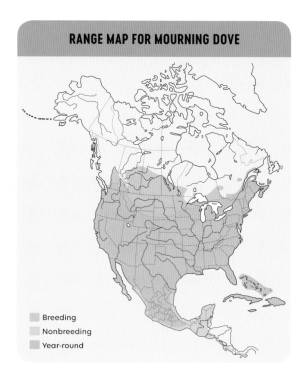

Breeding
Nonbreeding
Year-round

DUCK

WHAT IS A DUCK'S FAVORITE FOOD?
Quackers!

MALLARD

(*Anas platyrhynchos*)

FIELD MARKS: This familiar duck lives in fresh water everywhere—sometimes even swimming pools! In summer, males have shiny green heads, white neck rings, red-brown chests, curly tail feathers, and yellow bills. Females are brown. Both flash purple-blue wing patches in flight.

LENGTH: 23" (58 cm)

VOICE: As expected, Mallards say "*Quack*" . . . but only the females! Males make a quiet, raspy "*Queep.*"

FEEDING: Using their broad, flat bills, Mallards strain algae and other small water plants from lakes and ponds. When tipping forward to dabble for food, their bottoms stick straight up!

CONSERVATION: Like all water birds, Mallards can be poisoned by lead bullet pieces and fishing weights. A 1991 ban on lead shot for hunting water birds has helped populations grow.

HOW YOU CAN HELP: Encourage deer hunters to use copper bullets and fishermen to use tungsten fishing gear. Write to lawmakers asking them to ban lead products in natural areas.

Cool!
Mallards can fly 55 miles per hour (89 kph)! But each fall, they shed their flight feathers and can't fly for a whole month.

The female Mallard's brownish camouflage colors help protect her and her chicks.

RANGE MAP FOR MALLARD

Breeding
Nonbreeding
Year-round

(continued)

WOOD DUCK

(*Aix sponsa*)

FIELD MARKS: In breeding season, male Wood Ducks have bright colors and patterns, red eyes, and a swept-back, shiny green crest that looks like a helmet. Non-breeding males look similar to females, and they help rear the young.

LENGTH: 20" (51 cm)

VOICE: Males whistle "Jeeb." Females whistle "Oo-eeek."

FEEDING: Wood Ducks eat nuts, seeds, fruits, and aquatic insects.

CONSERVATION: These colorful ducks were over-hunted for food and feathers throughout the 1800s. Their wetland habitat and big nesting trees were also destroyed. Their numbers shrunk. Today, hunting limits and the use of nest boxes have helped Wood Ducks rebound.

HOW YOU CAN HELP: Protect forested wetlands; provide nest boxes there. Plant oak trees—Wood Ducks love acorns!

DID YOU KNOW? Wood Ducks nest in tree cavities and human-made nest boxes. So don't be surprised if you see this duck perched in a tree!

The male Wood Duck is colorful, while the female is brownish with a white teardrop eye ring. You might see Wood Ducks perching on tree limbs or flying through the woods.

A DUCK WALKS INTO A DRUG STORE AND BUYS LIPSTICK. THE CLERK ASKS, "CASH OR CREDIT CARD?" The duck says, "Just put it on my bill!"

WHAT HAPPENED TO THE DUCK WHO FLEW BACKWARD? She had a quack-up!

Cool!
Wood Duck chicks are superheroes! On "Jump Day," one-day-old chicks hear their mother call, sometimes from 50 feet (15 m) below the nest, and leap down to her. They may then walk more than a mile (1.6 km) to water. Then they learn to swim.

EAGLE

BALD EAGLE

(*Haliaeetus leucocephalus*)

FIELD MARKS: A Bald Eagle has a huge blackish-brown body and wings; pure white head and tail; yellow eyes, legs, feet; and a large, hooked yellow beak. Dark brown young can take five years to look like adults.

Fun Fact: The oldest known Bald Eagle was 38 years old.

LENGTH: 33" (84 cm)

VOICE: Several surprisingly weak, puppy-like, high-pitched, then falling notes.

FEEDING: Bald Eagles hunt on their own, but they also scavenge food, including dead animals, near wetlands. They also steal fish from Ospreys and gulls.

CONSERVATION: Just 12 years ago, Bald Eagles were an endangered species. Eating fish poisoned by a pesticide called DDT and being hunted by humans caused their decline. Banning eagle hunting and DDT has helped them recover. Lead poisoning is a current threat.

Cool! In 1782, the Bald Eagle became the national emblem of the United States.

HOW YOU CAN HELP: Protect tall trees where Bald Eagles build their giant stick nests. Avoid pesticides and lead ammunition.

SIMILAR SPECIES: Golden Eagles live in the western United States.

This Bald Eagle looks like it's about to land on the photographer! Fortunately, it landed on an overhead branch.

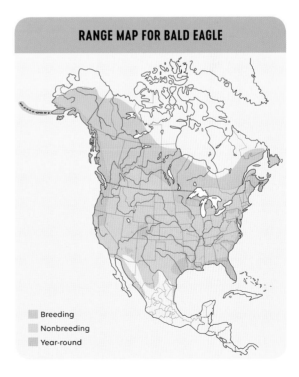

RANGE MAP FOR BALD EAGLE

Breeding
Nonbreeding
Year-round

FINCHES

HOUSE FINCH

(*Haemorhous mexicanus*)

FIELD MARKS: Males have a bright red forehead, face, and breast. Females are dull brown.

LENGTH: 5½" (14 cm)

VOICE: Long twittering song, often ending in "*Wheeeere*"

FEEDING: Eats mostly weed seeds, especially thistle and dandelion. Finches are the only songbirds to feed their chicks an all-seed diet. The seeds are pre-digested.

CONSERVATION: House Finches are abundant, but prone to a contagious eye disease (mycoplasmal conjunctivitis) that makes their eyes red and swollen and sometimes causes blindness.

HOW YOU CAN HELP: Help scientists track this disease by joining the Cornell Lab of Ornithology's Project FeederWatch. To avoid crowding, which can spread this disease, use several feeders spaced far apart and keep them clean.

Cool! Eastern House Finch populations got started around 1940 when New York pet store owners released their illegal West Coast finches to avoid arrest.

DID YOU KNOW? The male's color results from a varied diet. Females prefer older, more colorful males.

During courtship, the colorful male House Finch (right) feeds the female (left). He performs for her, too—flying up and then gliding back down, singing the whole time!

RANGE MAP FOR HOUSE FINCH

Year-round

AMERICAN GOLDFINCH

(*Spinus tristis*)

FIELD MARKS: Sunny yellow goldfinch males are a cheerful summer sight. They have black wings, tails, and foreheads. Females are a duller yellow-gray. The male sheds or molts his bright feathers in fall. Both sexes look similar in winter.

LENGTH: 4¾" (12 cm)

VOICE: "*Potato chip*" flight call

FEEDING: Goldfinches forage in twittering flocks, feeding almost entirely on seeds from flowering plants, grasses, and trees. They gobble up thistle seeds, then line their nests with the thistle fluff.

CONSERVATION: Goldfinches are abundant over much of North America.

Cool!

Goldfinches are among summer's last birds to nest and breed. The flower and weed seeds they eat, and the thistle fluff they use, are both more abundant in late summer.

HOW YOU CAN HELP: Plant native thistles, milkweed, and seed-bearing flowers such as sunflowers and coneflowers. Offer nyjer seed and black oil sunflower seeds at feeders.

PURPLE FINCH

(*Haemorhous purpureus*)

FIELD MARKS: Purple Finch males are a bright raspberry color (not purple, despite their name). Females are brown.

LENGTH: 6" (15 cm)

VOICE: Males sing warbling songs for different purposes. When flocking, they may sing more than 25 notes in one song.

FEEDING: Purple Finches have a varied diet: seeds from trees such as pines, elms, and maples; flower buds, berries, fruits, and insects, too.

CONSERVATION: These chunky finches breed in evergreen forests. Habitat loss and competition from House Finches and House Sparrows have caused Purple Finch populations to decline.

HOW YOU CAN HELP: Plant native evergreen trees and offer black oil sunflower seeds at feeders.

This American Goldfinch pair (female left, male right) enjoys a birdbath. Goldfinches are among the last birds to breed in summer.

The Purple Finch's cone-shaped bill is perfect for grabbing sunflower seeds.

CANADA GOOSE

(*Branta canadensis*)

FIELD MARKS: This goose has a large brownish body and a light chest and rump. A wide, white chin strap divides its black head and long black neck.

LENGTH: 25"–45" (64–114 m). Southern geese are larger.

VOICE: Canada Geese honk loudly! They also hiss to protect their nests.

FEEDING: Geese dabble for vegetation in water. They also graze on grassy lawns, grain crops, and berries.

CONSERVATION: Common and increasing. Some people object to goose droppings on golf courses or in parks. Others enjoy seeing geese up close.

HOW YOU CAN HELP: If geese are nesting nearby, enjoy watching the parents protect and raise their little yellow goslings.

DID YOU KNOW? Migrating geese often fly in a V shape to better fly and communicate with each other.

SIMILAR SPECIES: Among the many goose species that exist, there's now a new goose! The smaller Cackling Goose was considered a type of Canada Goose until 2005. Scientists have now proved they are separate species.

Fun Fact:
Canada Geese mate for life.

Canada Geese vary in size and color, depending on where they live. Darker geese are found further west.

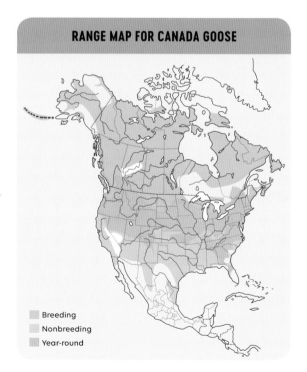

RANGE MAP FOR CANADA GOOSE

Breeding
Nonbreeding
Year-round

GULL

WHAT DO YOU CALL SEAGULLS THAT LIVE BY THE BAY? Bay-gulls (bagels)!

HERRING GULL

(*Larus argentatus*)

FIELD MARKS: A Herring Gull has a white body, gray back and wings, black wingtips, pink legs, and a yellow bill with a red spot. Brownish youngsters take four years to look like adults.

LENGTH: 24" (61 cm)

VOICE: Cries "*Ha ha ha!*" and "*Ke-ow!*"

FEEDING: Gulls eat everything! That includes fish, shellfish, and lots of discarded human food at landfills.

CONSERVATION: By 1900, Herring Gulls had been overhunted for their feathers, which were used to decorate women's hats. A 1918 law made hunting migratory birds illegal and helped save them. Today overfishing, the closing of landfills, and oil pollution are reducing Herring Gull populations.

HOW YOU CAN HELP: Eat sustainably caught seafood. Help keep oceans clean.

DID YOU KNOW? Gull chicks peck the red spot on a parent's lower beak to get a pre-digested dinner. Yum!

SIMILAR SPECIES: Great Black-backed Gulls, the world's largest gulls, have about a five-foot (1.5 m) wingspan!

Cool!
Herring Gulls fly up high and drop shellfish on rocks below. When the shells crack, it's chow time!

In winter, Herring Gulls are found along most U.S. coastlines.

RANGE MAP FOR HERRING GULL

Breeding
Migration
Winter
Year-round

HAWK

RED-TAILED HAWK

(*Buteo jamaicensis*)

FIELD MARKS: Not surprisingly, Red-tailed Hawks have reddish tails! They are often brown above and pale below, but colors vary.

LENGTH: 22" (56 cm)

VOICE: Piercing scream that rises then falls: "*Keeeeeeerrr!*"

FEEDING: These birds of prey eat various small mammals, especially mice and rats. They also eat other birds, reptiles, and recently killed animals.

CONSERVATION: Where prey is plentiful, Red-tails thrive, even in cities. The most common large hawk, they're still threatened by eating poisoned rodents and carrion containing lead.

HOW YOU CAN HELP: Preserve tall trees and open areas where Red-tails hunt. Avoid lead ammunition and rodenticides. Teach others how these hawks provide natural pest control.

DID YOU KNOW? Since 1972, the Migratory Bird Treaty Act has included protection for hawks and eagles.

OTHER HAWKS: Cooper's and Sharp-shinned Hawks visit bird feeders—but not for seeds!

Cool!
The Red-tails' "*Keeeeeeerrr!*" call is often used in movies, television shows, and commercials. Listen for it!

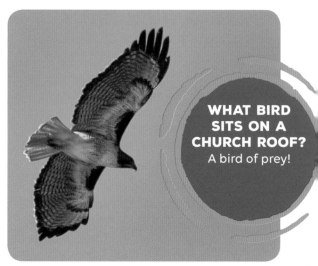

WHAT BIRD SITS ON A CHURCH ROOF?
A bird of prey!

A Red-tailed Hawk soars over California's Central Coast.

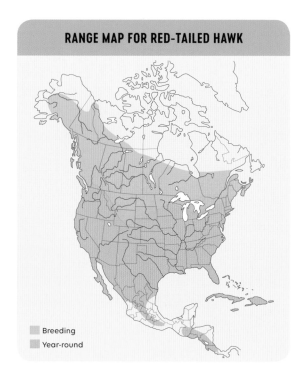

RANGE MAP FOR RED-TAILED HAWK

Breeding
Year-round

HERON

GREAT BLUE HERON

(*Ardea herodias*)

FIELD MARKS: The Great Blue Heron is a large blue-gray bird with a long neck, long bill, long plumes, and long legs. It flies in slow-motion, with neck tucked and legs trailing.

VOICE: Loud, croaky "*Grak!*"

LENGTH: 48" (122 cm)

FEEDING: This heron stalks prey, including fish, frogs, birds, and small mammals. It stands motionless in shallow water until prey approaches, then strikes with lightning speed!

CONSERVATION: Often nests in large colonies. Widespread, but threatened by habitat loss, polluted water, and human disturbance.

HOW YOU CAN HELP: Help preserve wetlands and the standing dead trees these herons need for nesting. Where trees are scarce, some caring groups have put up artificial trees with nesting platforms.

DID YOU KNOW? These herons use "powder down" from their chest feathers to clean and waterproof themselves.

SIMILAR SPECIES: The Little Blue Heron is half the size of the Great Blue.

Fun Fact:
Herons flip fish before eating them so they go down headfirst—sharp fins avoided! The heron's neck bulges as the still-alive fish slides slowly down.

Long legs allow Great Blue Herons to stand tall.

RANGE MAP FOR GREAT BLUE HERON

Breeding
Nonbreeding
Year-round

HUMMINGBIRD

RUBY-THROATED HUMMINGBIRD

(Archilochus colubris)

FIELD MARKS: The male's throat glitters ruby red in sunlight. Females' throats are white. Both have green backs.

LENGTH: 3¼" (8 cm)

VOICE: High, twittering "*Chee-dit*" calls. The "humming" is the sound of their wings beating 53 times a second!

FEEDING: Hummers use their long, thin beaks to sip nectar from tube-shaped flowers, especially orange and red ones. They also sip sap from tree holes drilled by sapsuckers, a type of woodpecker. And they hunt tiny insects such as fruit flies and mosquitos.

CONSERVATION: The only Eastern hummingbird, Ruby-throats are abundant.

HOW YOU CAN HELP: Plant coral honeysuckle, cardinal flower, trumpet vine, and other hummer-friendly plants.

DID YOU KNOW? Hummingbird eggs are the size of peas.

SIMILAR SPECIES: Eastern states normally host only Ruby-throated Hummingbirds. Western states host many more species, including Anna's and Rufous Hummingbirds.

Fun Fact: Hummingbirds breathe more than 140 times per minute! Can you?

Cool! Unlike other birds, hummers can fly backward.

A male Ruby-throated Hummingbird shows off his flying skills. He may fly non-stop during migration to and from Mexico and Central America for up to 20 hours.

RANGE MAP FOR RUBY-THROATED HUMMINGBIRD

Breeding

Migration

Nonbreeding

JAY

BLUE JAY
(*Cyanocitta cristata*)

FIELD MARKS: Blue Jays are various shades of blue, including the head and crest. They have white wing bars, white tips on wings and tail, a light gray breast, and a black "necklace."

LENGTH: 11" (28 cm)

VOICE: Loud "*Jay*" and "*Jeer*" calls may signal danger. Jays also buzz, whistle, and imitate other birds, especially hawks.

FEEDING: Acorns are a favorite food. Insects, spiders, nuts, seeds, bird eggs, and small vertebrates are also on the menu.

CONSERVATION: Widespread throughout the eastern and central United States.

HOW YOU CAN HELP: At feeders, provide big seeds such as striped sunflower and peanuts—either shelled or unshelled.

SIMILAR SPECIES: Over a dozen jay species call the U.S. home. Slightly larger Steller's Jays, as well as scrub-jays, are found out west, except for the Florida Scrub-Jay.

Cool!
Jays bury acorns to eat later—but often they don't come back for them. When lots of uneaten acorns grow into big oak trees, thank the jays for planting oak forests!

WHAT BIRD IS A LETTER?
A jay!

Blue Jays are in the same family as other highly intelligent birds like crows and magpies.

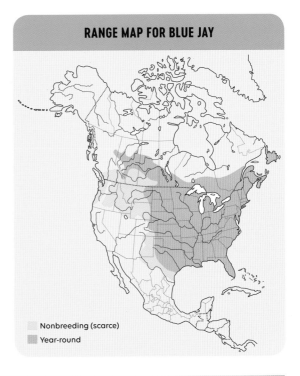

RANGE MAP FOR BLUE JAY

Nonbreeding (scarce)
Year-round

JUNCO

DARK-EYED JUNCO

(Junco hyemalis)

FIELD MARKS: Juncos are generally dark gray or brown back, with a whitish belly and tiny pinkish beak. Colors vary by location. The white outer tail feathers flash as they fly.

LENGTH: 6½" (17 cm)

VOICE: Song is a musical, single-pitched trill: "*Titititit!*"

FEEDING: Juncos eat thousands of weed seeds daily. They need lots of energy to survive winter temperatures.

CONSERVATION: Although Juncos are numerous, their populations decline slightly each year.

HOW YOU CAN HELP: Brush piles and shrubs provide good winter cover. Offer cracked corn, millet, and shelled sunflower seeds or chips—either on the ground or in tray feeders. Juncos' tiny beaks are perfect for picking up weed seeds, but too small for whole sunflower seeds.

DID YOU KNOW? Juncos are sometimes called "snowbirds," as they often appear at feeders during snowstorms. Their colors also remind people of winter: gray skies above, snowy below!

Cool!
Juncos prefer cool weather. They are among the most common winter visitors at bird feeders.

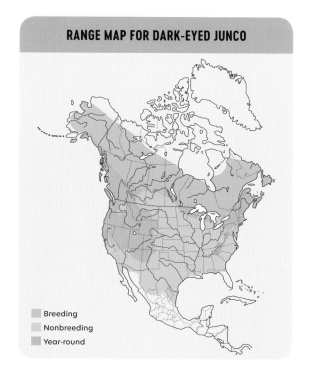

During courtship, male juncos show off to potential mates. If a female likes what she sees, she starts building a nest.

RANGE MAP FOR DARK-EYED JUNCO

- Breeding
- Nonbreeding
- Year-round

NUTHATCH

WHITE-BREASTED NUTHATCH

(*Sitta carolinensis*)

FIELD MARKS: This nuthatch is named for its white breast. Males have black crowns; females have gray crowns. Both have white faces.

LENGTH: 5½" (14 cm)

VOICE: Song is a series of soft whistled calls on one pitch: "*Whi-whi-whi-whi-whi-whi-whi.*" Call is an excited, nasal "*Yank-yank-yank!*"

FEEDING: Nuthatches eat acorns, beechnuts, and insects picked from tree trunks. They also cache (hide) sunflower seeds from feeders.

CONSERVATION: Common and widespread

HOW YOU CAN HELP: Nuthatches often nest in abandoned woodpecker tree cavities. Protect deciduous forests and standing dead trees. Stock feeders with suet, hulled peanuts, peanut butter, and both shelled and unshelled sunflower seeds. Hang nest boxes and drill starter holes in dead trees.

DID YOU KNOW? Nuthatches usually mate for life.

SIMILAR SPECIES: Red-breasted Nuthatches have rusty underparts, and are found in coniferous forests.

Fun Fact: Nuthatches have the unique habit of walking head-first down large tree trunks, searching for food.

Down the tree we go! The White-breasted Nuthatch's head-first habit inspired its nickname: "Tree Mouse."

RANGE MAP FOR WHITE-BREASTED NUTHATCH

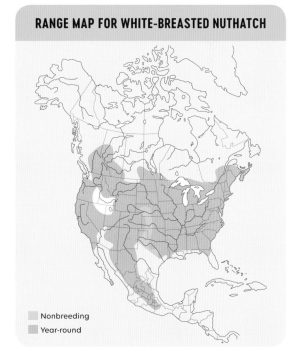

Nonbreeding
Year-round

OWL

"KNOCK, KNOCK." **"WHO'S THERE?"** "Great Horned Owl, that's *hoo-hoo-hoo!*"

GREAT HORNED OWL

(*Bubo virginianus*)

FIELD MARKS: A Great Horned Owl has a large gray-brown body, white throat, striped breast, and big yellow eyes. The "horns" are actually feathered ear tufts, giving this owl a cat-like look!

LENGTH: 22" (56 cm)

VOICE: Deep hoots: "*Hoo-hoo-hoo, hoo-hoo!*" Pairs hoot together; the male's voice is lower, even though he is smaller than the female.

FEEDING: These powerful nighttime predators fly on silent wings. They swoop on all kinds of prey, including other owls and animals as large as skunks!

CONSERVATION: Although they're North America's most widespread owl, Great Horned Owls are declining, threatened by logging and pesticide-poisoned prey.

HOW YOU CAN HELP: Help protect old trees where owls nest. Avoid pesticides.

SIMILAR SPECIES: Other "eared" owls include the Long-eared Owl and the much smaller Eastern and Western screech-owls. The Barred Owl lacks ear tufts. Its main predator is the Great Horned Owl!

Cool! Like other owls, the Great Horned can turn its head more than halfway around its body!

Fun Fact: These owls lay eggs in mid-winter. They often take over hawk or eagle nests.

The Great Horned Owl is found in nearly all North and South American habitats. Its powerful hunting skills have earned it the nickname "Tiger Owl."

RANGE MAP FOR GREAT HORNED OWL

Year-round
Year-round (scarce)

ROBIN

AMERICAN ROBIN

(*Turdus migratorius*)

FIELD MARKS: Robins have a dark gray-brown back; reddish-orange breast; white eye ring; blackish head, neck, and tail; and yellow bill. Females are usually paler.

LENGTH: 10" (25 cm)

VOICE: A clear, musical song with repeated short rising and falling phrases: "*Cheerolee, cheery, cheeryup!*" Sharp call: "*Tuk!*"

FEEDING: Robins eat small tree fruits and shrub berries. They also eat insects, snails, and earthworms in warmer weather.

CONSERVATION: Abundant. Because American Robins often feed on lawns, they're susceptible to pesticide poisoning.

HOW YOU CAN HELP: Robins need big trees for nesting and singing, and pesticide-free lawns for foraging. Sumac, crabapple, and hawthorn trees provide robins with fruit in early spring. Put up nesting shelves under porch and barn eaves.

DID YOU KNOW? Robins are considered a cheery sign of spring. But breeding robins are so territorial, they may attack their own reflections!

Fun Fact:
Robins on lawns tip their heads and seem to be listening for prey— but those earthworms are located by sight, not sound.

Some American Robins migrate for the winter; others don't. Some large winter flocks seem to follow the food.

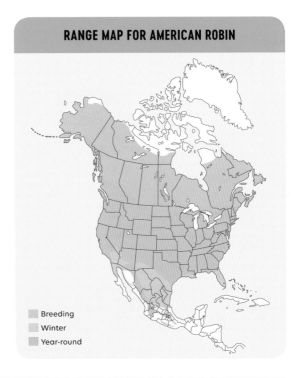

RANGE MAP FOR AMERICAN ROBIN

Breeding
Winter
Year-round

SPARROWS

SONG SPARROW

(*Melospiza melodia*)

FIELD MARKS: A Song Sparrow has a brown back and streaky breast; the streaks converge into a large central dark spot. The size and color vary depending on where it lives. It dips its tail in flight.

LENGTH: 6" (15 cm) average

VOICE: A melodious song begins with several "*Sweet sweet sweet*" notes, followed by jumbled whistles and trills. Males often sing out in the open at eye level.

FEEDING: Ground-feeding Song Sparrows eat weed seeds and insects. During summer, insects make up half their diet, along with seeds and berries.

CONSERVATION: Common and widespread but declining in areas where they depend on tidal marsh habitat. Mostly absent from arid regions, including southern California and southwestern Arizona.

HOW YOU CAN HELP: Protect fields with scattered shrubs and thickets. Build brush piles to attract these birds. Offer birdseed such as white proso millet and cracked corn in tray feeders.

DID YOU KNOW? Song Sparrows' nests often host Brown-headed Cowbirds. This bird lays its eggs in the nests of other birds. The cowbird chicks often out-compete the sparrow chicks for food.

Cool!
In winter, Song Sparrows can eat several thousand tiny seeds per hour! They need the calories to survive.

This Song Sparrow is doing what it's known for: singing its song! Their songs vary slightly by region.

RANGE MAP FOR SONG SPARROW

Breeding
Nonbreeding
Year-round

WHAT BIRD IS AN EXTRA PART OF THE GARDEN?
A "spare row" (sparrow)!

CHIPPING SPARROW

(Spizella passerina)

FIELD MARKS: Chipping Sparrows have a bright reddish cap, black line through the eye, white eyebrow stripe, brown back, and light gray, unmarked breast. It's duller in winter.

LENGTH: 5¼" (13 cm)

VOICE: Song is a long, insect-like trill. Call is a sharp "Chip!"

FEEDING: Chipping Sparrows feed constantly on grass and weed seeds on the ground. They capture insects to feed young.

CONSERVATION: Common but declining slightly. "Chippies" have adapted to backyard gardens and farms, especially where they find tall trees, shrubs, and lawns.

HOW YOU CAN HELP: Weedy garden edges attract these tiny sparrows. Offer black oil sunflower seeds at platform feeders, and mixed seed, including white proso millet, on the ground.

Male Chipping Sparrows sing about 55 "chip" notes in under 4 seconds! Described as trilling, this song is commonly heard in spring.

DID YOU KNOW? Chippies often seem tame, letting humans come close.

SIMILAR SPECIES: Larger American Tree Sparrows have a dark breast spot.

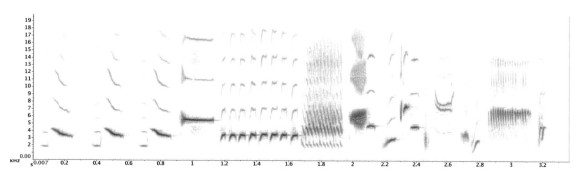

This spectrogram shows the first three clear notes sung by a Maryland Song Sparrow, followed by whistles and trills. Ornithologists use spectrograms, or sonograms, to "see" bird sounds.

TREE SWALLOW

(*Tachycineta bicolor*)

FIELD MARKS: These acrobatic flyers are blue-green above and snowy white below.

LENGTH: 5½" (14 cm)

VOICE: Song a musical "*Tee a weet*" with variations

FEEDING: Tree Swallows eat mostly flying insects; they also eat berries and seeds in winter.

CONSERVATION: Tree Swallows are still common, but populations have declined. Their high-insect diet exposes them to pesticides. Tree cavities where they once nested have become rarer.

HOW YOU CAN HELP: In early spring, put up bluebird-size nest boxes. Hang baskets of feathers. Tree Swallows use them to line their nests.

DID YOU KNOW? Tree Swallows regularly nest in nest boxes next to bluebirds—but not next to each other!

SIMILAR SPECIES: Barn Swallows have a long forked tail and are orange below and blue-black above. They can drink and bathe while flying. This talent comes in handy during their long migration—sometimes 7,000 miles (11,265 km)!

WHY DO BIRDS FLY SOUTH IN THE WINTER?
Because it's too far to walk!

Male Tree Swallows are steely blue or green above, with bright white feathers below. Females are duller.

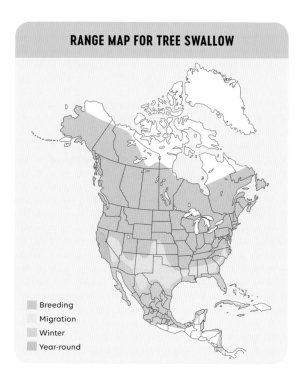

RANGE MAP FOR TREE SWALLOW

Breeding
Migration
Winter
Year-round

TURKEY

WILD TURKEY

(*Meleagris gallopavo*)

FIELD MARKS: These large, dark-brownish birds have bald heads and pink legs. Males have bright red, fleshy wattles hanging from their "chins." They fan out their tail feathers to impress the smaller females during courtship. (Domestic turkeys are white.)

LENGTH: 3½' (107 cm)

VOICE: Males make the familiar "*Gobble.*" Females call "*Tuk!*" to their chicks.

FEEDING: Turkeys scratch through leafy forest floors for acorns and insects.

CONSERVATION: Widespread, but in patches. Wild Turkeys were nearly wiped out by over-hunting and habitat destruction by the 1900s. Habitat restoration and reintroduction programs have since boosted their numbers.

HOW YOU CAN HELP: Plant native oaks—turkeys love acorns! Make leaf piles so they can forage. Grit helps turkeys digest their food, so put out a bowl of sand or fine gravel.

DID YOU KNOW? Turkeys roost in trees at night.

Cool!
Legend says that Benjamin Franklin suggested the Wild Turkey as the emblem of the United States. It lost to the Bald Eagle.

Wild Turkeys can swim! They pull in their wings, fan out their tails, and start kicking.

RANGE MAP FOR WILD TURKEY

Year-round

VULTURE

TURKEY VULTURE

(Cathartes aura)

FIELD MARKS: The Turkey Vulture has a red, un-feathered head, ivory bill, and brownish-black body. From below, its wings appear two-toned: black in front, silver-gray behind. Flying Turkey Vultures hold their wings in a V shape. Wingtip feathers are spread out like fingers.

LENGTH: 2' (61 cm).

VOICE: Hisses when eating or annoyed.

FEEDING: Turkey Vultures are nature's "clean-up crew." They eat dead animals (carrion), often feasting on roadkill.

CONSERVATION: Although they are abundant, Turkey Vultures can get lead poisoning from feeding on dead animals shot with lead bullets.

HOW YOU CAN HELP: Support lead-free ammunition.

In flight, Turkey Vultures characteristically teeter from side to side as they soar.

DID YOU KNOW? Turkey Vultures use their fine-tuned sense of smell to find dead animals.

SIMILAR SPECIES: Black Vultures are slightly smaller and can't smell as well as Turkey Vultures.

Fun Fact:
If Turkey Vultures are disturbed, they may throw up on the intruder. Vulture vomit is an effective repellent!

RANGE MAP FOR TURKEY VULTURE

Breeding
Year-round

WOODPECKERS

DOWNY WOODPECKER

(*Dryobates pubescens*)

FIELD MARKS: The smallest U.S. woodpecker, the Downy is a bundle of black and white—except for a small red patch behind the male's head. They have spotted wings, a white back and undersides, and a relatively small bill.

LENGTH: 6½" (17 cm)

VOICE: Calls include a high-pitched "*Pik*" or "*Peek!*"

FEEDING: Woodpeckers forage for insects on tree trunk surfaces. They also eat acorns and berries.

CONSERVATION: Common throughout most of the United States

HOW YOU CAN HELP: Help protect the dead trees that these woodpeckers and other cavity-nesting birds need for nesting. At feeders, offer suet, peanuts, and black oil sunflower seeds.

DID YOU KNOW? Extra stiff tail feathers help woodpeckers steady themselves on tree trunks.

SIMILAR SPECIES: The larger, bigger-billed Hairy Woodpecker is often mistaken for a Downy.

Fun Fact:
Woodpecker skulls and beaks have built-in shock absorbers. This lets them hammer without headaches!

Cool!
Woodpeckers' loud drumming on wooden or metal surfaces says, "Territory taken!"

Both male and female Downy Woodpeckers drum on dead trees to attract mates or claim a territory.

RANGE MAP FOR DOWNY WOODPECKER

Year-round

(continued)

PILEATED WOODPECKER

(*Dryocopus pileatus*)

FIELD MARKS: This largest living U.S. woodpecker is easy to recognize by its bright red triangular crest. It has black and white stripes on its face and neck; the male has a red cheek stripe. The female cheek stripe is black. The up-and-down flight shows white underwings.

LENGTH: 16½" (42 cm)

VOICE: Long, loud call sounds like someone laughing: "*Yuk-yuk-yuk!*"

FEEDING: Pileated Woodpeckers dig into rotten wood with their strong bills to feast on ants, grubs, and other insects. They create rectangular holes, often seen in forest trees. They eat fruit, too.

CONSERVATION: These woodpeckers declined sharply when Eastern forests were cleared in the 1800s. As the forests returned, so did they.

HOW YOU CAN HELP: Help preserve large dead trees and logs.

DID YOU KNOW? The voice of the Woody Woodpecker cartoon character is modeled on the Pileated Woodpecker. "Ha-ha-ha-HA-ha!"

A Pileated Woodpecker home, which is used for only one season, can take six weeks to chisel out. Many other creatures are happy to move in once they depart.

Cool!
Pairs hammer out a new nest cavity each season. Abandoned nests become homes for other birds.

A female Pileated Woodpecker grabs a high-fat meal at a backyard suet feeder. Note her black cheek stripe, which distinguishes her from the male.

WHAT DID THE TREE SAY TO THE WOODPECKER?
"Wood you please leaf me alone!"

WREN

HOUSE WREN

(*Troglodytes aedon*)

FIELD MARKS: House Wrens have a brown body and narrow black bars on their wings and tail; the tail is often cocked.

LENGTH: 4¾" (12 cm)

VOICE: Loud, bubbly song

FEEDING: House Wrens are a gardener's best friend! They feed almost entirely on insects, including grasshoppers, beetles, and caterpillars.

CONSERVATION: Widespread and abundant.

HOW YOU CAN HELP: Put up nest boxes with 1¼" (3 cm) entrance holes; wrens will gladly fill them with their twig nests. Create a brush pile from small branches to attract them.

DID YOU KNOW? House Wrens make up in feistiness what they lack in size! They may attack much larger birds and they can destroy other species' nests when competing for nest sites.

SIMILAR SPECIES: Carolina Wrens visit feeders and sing "*Tea-kettle, tea-kettle!*" They have a white throat, reddish-brown back, and white eye stripe.

Fun Fact:
Male House Wrens start multiple nests, often in odd locations such as flowerpots, mailboxes, or shoes! Later-arriving females choose a male and one of his nests by adding a soft lining.

Wrens are tiny birds with big, loud songs!

RANGE MAP FOR HOUSE WREN

- Breeding
- Migration
- Nonbreeding
- Year-round

COMMON NONNATIVE BIRDS

(Rock Pigeon, House Sparrow, European Starling, Parrots)

Many birds in the United States are not native; that is, they were not found here until after European settlement. Yet they thrive. Generally, nonnative birds have been deliberately introduced, were pet birds that escaped, or spread from surrounding countries into North America. What follows are profiles and photos of some of the nonnative species you are likely to see.

ROCK PIGEON

(*Columba livia*)

FIELD MARKS: Often simply called pigeons, these birds come in many colors and patterns. One common form has a dark head, gray body, and two dark wing bars. Neck feathers gleam iridescent purple and green.

VOICE: A soft "*Coo roo coo*"

LENGTH: 13" (33 cm)

FEEDING: Rock Pigeons eat seeds, grains, and lots of thrown-away human food.

CONSERVATION: Widespread. Pigeons have helped restore Peregrine Falcon populations, especially in cities, where falcons feed on them.

HOW YOU CAN HELP: Appreciate the pigeon's beauty, adaptability, and 6,000-year-old history with humans.

DID YOU KNOW? Trained pigeons carried messages in ancient Rome and for the U.S. Army in World Wars I and II.

Rock Pigeons' plumage varies. This "blue bar"—two black bands on blue-gray wings—is the most common plumage.

SIMILAR SPECIES: Nonnative Eurasian Collared-Doves have a narrow black band behind their necks—the "collar." Since 1982, these birds have spread rapidly across North America.

Cool!
Rock Pigeons, named for rocky cliffs where they nested in their native Europe, have adapted to using tall city buildings instead.

HOUSE SPARROW

(Passer domesticus)

FIELD MARKS: This familiar "sparrow" of cities, suburbs, and farms is a dark streaky brown. Males have white cheeks and a black bib.

LENGTH: 6" (15 cm)

VOICE: Song consists of constantly repeated chirps. Calls include rattles and whistles.

FEEDING: House Sparrows eat mostly seeds; sometimes they also eat insects and fruit.

CONSERVATION: House Sparrows were first introduced in Brooklyn, New York in 1850 to control city insects. These adaptable birds have now spread throughout North America and they are abundant. They nest in tree holes and nest boxes, often competing with native songbirds for cavities.

HOW YOU CAN HELP: House Sparrows are flourishing, no doubt helped by bird feeders. Surprisingly, they have declined rapidly in their native England, where efforts are being made to restore them.

DID YOU KNOW? House Sparrows are not actually sparrows! They are members of the Eurasian weaver-finch family.

Stout House Sparrow bills are good for hulling seeds. The male's beak color varies from black to grayish or yellow.

Fun Fact:
House Sparrows thrive even in the densest downtown city areas. They are never far from humans!

EUROPEAN STARLING

(*Sturnus vulgaris*)

FIELD MARKS: As spring approaches, starlings turn from white-speckled to black with a glossy green and purple sheen. Their bills change from dark to yellow. Their legs are pinkish-brown.

LENGTH: 8½" (22 cm)

VOICE: A mix of rattles, squeaks, whistles, and the mimicked calls of other species.

FEEDING: Starlings' adaptability and big appetites become obvious as they descend on feeders and fruit trees in large numbers. These omnivores also eat earthworms, insects, spiders, and berries.

CONSERVATION: Introduced in New York City's Central Park in 1890, starlings are now widespread from coast to coast in cities, parks, and farms—wherever there are humans! They often compete for nesting cavities with native birds.

HOW YOU CAN HELP: Starlings are abundant—they don't need much help! However, they are listed as threatened in their native Great Britain.

From the 100 starlings released in New York's Central Park over a century ago, starling populations have now grown to an estimated 200 million.

Cool!
After molting each summer, the starling's new white-tipped feathers against its black body create a starry look that gives this bird its name.

PARROTS IN AMERICA

Nonnative parrots are becoming more common in the United States. Data from the Christmas Bird Count and eBird show that up to 56 different parrot species have been seen in 43 states. Many are breeding—making nests and raising chicks. California, Florida, and Texas have the biggest parrot populations. Monk Parakeets and Red-crowned Amazon parrots are most numerous.

The great 2003 documentary *The Wild Parrots of Telegraph Hill*, produced by Judy Irving, tells the story of San Francisco's wild parrots.

This Red-crowned Parrot's native home is in the lowlands of northeastern Mexico. Its numbers are increasing in the U.S.

2 OUTSIDE WITH THE BIRDS:

GAMES, ACTIVITIES, AND ADVENTURES

Where are the birds? Outside, of course. So, outside is the best place to look for them! This chapter will help you prepare for and begin taking bird walks. This is the best way to find out which birds are where. Chances are, you'll get to see and hear a lot of birds!

Then take things further by learning to use binoculars. It's the best way to see birds up close. You can also start identifying birds by learning bird songs.

This chapter will also help you bring birds closer by attracting them with water and food. A focus on growing native plants to feed and fuel birds wraps up this section. What's more beautiful than an American Goldfinch on a bright yellow sunflower head . . . or a jewel-like hummingbird darting among bright red nectar-filled flowers? How lucky we are to watch, care for, and learn from wild birds!

DINOSAURS AND BIRDS

"Hope is the thing with feathers," wrote poet Emily Dickinson. And today, *only* birds have feathers. But research shows that many dinosaurs had feathers, too—maybe even the huge theropod, *Tyrannosaurus rex!* Theropods also had hollow bones, just like modern birds. In a way, today's birds are living dinosaurs! That's fun to think about when you're outside watching birds.

↢ Canada Geese build their nests on the ground near water. Males guard the nest, hissing out threats to intruders. Females incubate the eggs, then brood their tiny yellow goslings.

TAKE A BIRD WALK

Who are your bird neighbors? One way to find out is to go on a bird walk! It all starts with getting outside and paying attention. Get familiar with the birds you might see where you live. Notice how they look and when they're in your area. For recent sightings, you can go online to eBird (ebird.org) or research local bird checklists.

Next, plan your own walk with your friends or family, or join a bird club or nature center walk. Organized walks will help you become a better birder by learning from more experienced birders. You'll also meet fellow birdwatchers.

NOTE TO PARENTS: Longer group bird walks might not work well for younger children. Instead, try exploring a smaller setting, such as a backyard.

ACTIVITY

Help everyone learn to observe. Ask: Who sees a bird? What's it doing? If you're joining others on a walk, there are a few things that will help you see and hear more:

- **Use indoor voices.** Or, better yet, whisper! Try not to yell, "Look at that!" Loud noises startle birds.
- **Make gentle movements.** Sudden movements startle birds, too.
- **Wear nature-colored clothing.** Subtle greens, grays, and browns help you blend into bird habitat. Whites and bright colors make you stand out.
- **Humans only!** Leave dogs at home. Even quiet ones scare birds away.

Record the birds you see in your notebook, along with the date, time, location, weather, and notes on things such as odd plumage or behavior. You've started a Birder's Life List! Compare your list with other peoples' lists. Did you see the same things?

MATERIALS

- Bird identification field guide (book, app, or online)
- Binoculars (if you have them) to zoom in on birds
- Pencil and notebook to record birds you see and hear

DISCOVERIES

Discover more birds by bird-walking during spring and fall migration times, and in the early mornings. These are all "peak" times to "peek" at birds! Who knew there were so many kinds of birds living nearby?

FOLLOW UP

Keep on bird-walking! Try visiting different habitats to see different birds. Or try the same walk again and see whether you notice anything new.

Bird walks are full of surprises—like this White-breasted Nuthatch's fierce territorial display.

At Audubon's Discovery Center in Philadelphia, educator Keith Russell helps birders spot birds using a tree like a clock face—a bird in a treetop above the trunk is at 12 o'clock.

BIRDS THROUGH BINOCULARS

If you want to find birds, you'll need to learn to think like one! And if you want to see birds up close, you'll need to learn to use binoculars. All it takes is practice. Using binoculars will become quick and easy in no time. You'll be surprised at how much you see.

MATERIALS

+ Binoculars with binocular strap

TIP: No need to spend money on brand-new binoculars. Free hand-me-downs in good condition work fine.

ACTIVITY

Follow these steps to learn your way around binoculars:

1. **Strap it.** Put the strap around your neck so the binoculars (a.k.a. bins) won't fall to the ground.

2. **Get the right fit.** Look at a non-moving object such as a street sign. Keep your eyes on the sign without moving your head. Holding the sides of your binoculars with both hands, slowly lift them to your eyes. What do you see?

   If you see dark shadows or blackness, stop! The two cylinders, or barrels, are either too close together or too far apart for your eyes. Look through the eyepieces while moving the barrels in and out at the center hinge until the blackness disappears. Now you've got a good fit.

3. **Time to focus.** View the sign again through your binoculars. Then turn the center focus knob. The sign should get sharper, fuzzier, and sharper again as you move the knob. Now you can get focused!

Hog Island Audubon Camp instructor Anna Tucker helps a camper adjust her binoculars.

4. **For your eyes only.** Look through the bins again. Close your right eye and look through your left eye. Turn the center focus knob until you see a crisp, clear image. Now switch—close your left eye and look at the sign with your right eye. Usually the right eyepiece has another focus knob (the diopter). Adjust this knob until you see the sign clearly with your right eye.

Tip:
Look at the bird first, not your field guide. Birds fly away. Field guides usually don't!

(continued)

5. **Focus both eyes.** Now, with both eyes open, look through the eyepieces. If things aren't in focus, repeat step 4.

Still seeing black edges? Adjust the eyecups. The usual twist-up position creates distance between your eye and the eyepiece. If you wear glasses, twist the eyecups down.

6. **Find a bird!** Keeping the bird in view, without moving your head, lift the binoculars to your eyes to re-spot it.

DISCOVERIES

Once you get the hang of using binoculars—and you soon will—a whole new world will open for you!

FOLLOW UP

Take care of your binoculars. Keep them away from mud, sand, and saltwater. Clean the lenses regularly with a soft brush, then a soft cloth.

BIRD SPOTTING TIPS

Find more birds by thinking like a bird! Ask yourself some bird-centered questions:

♦ **ARE THERE GOOD PERCHES?** These include fence posts, bare tree limbs, power lines, rooftop ridges, big sunflowers, and hummingbird vines. Birds such as bluebirds, flycatchers, and raptors that hunt by sight often perch and watch for prey. Hummingbirds use the same perch time after time.

♦ **IS THERE A FIELD TO SOAR OVER?** Birds such as vultures and eagles fly high to search for food. Many kinds of birds take to the skies during migration. Always look up!

♦ **WHAT'S THIS HABITAT?** Think about what you, as a bird, would need to live. Different birds live in different habitats. Forests are chickadee, titmouse, and woodpecker territory. Is there a lake or pond where you're birding? Look for ducks, Great Blue Herons, and other birds seeking a swim, food, or a drink.

At dusk, after birding for over 13 hours in Cape May County, New Jersey, joyful young Maryland birders celebrate winning their division of the 2019 World Series of Birding! They spotted 105 different bird species.

DO-IT-YOURSELF BIRDBATH

Water makes all life possible, including bird life. If you want a surefire way to draw some birds to your yard and practice your binocular skills, give them a birdbath! During heat waves, offering water can even save birds' lives. At other times you can enjoy watching them drinking, bathing, and splashing.

ACTIVITY

For most birds, many store-bought birdbaths are too steep and too deep. For a budget birdbath that's just right, place your shallow lid or saucer at ground level, preferably in the shade. Press it into a pre-made bed of sand, gravel, or both. Don't put the birdbath too close to bushes or other cover—predators can hide there.

Add water, but to no more than 3" (8 cm) deep. You can add a large, flat rock for weight and grip. Then retreat and observe the birds!

DISCOVERIES

Birds such as robins, warblers, and hawks don't usually visit feeders. But they love birdbaths!

FOLLOW UP

Clean your birdbath often with a scrub brush—especially in hot weather. Avoid detergents or disinfectants. Keep birdbaths full, fresh, and clean. Adding ice on warm days ensures a ready supply of melting fresh water.

MATERIALS

- Shallow (about 2" [5 cm] deep), sturdy, leak-proof garbage can lid, or large flowerpot saucer (sturdy plastic or glazed ceramic holds water best)

- Sand, gravel, or both

- Water

- Large rock (optional)

Setting up a birdbath is as easy as filling a shallow plastic flower pot saucer. Nearby rocks for birds to land on and flowers for hummers to sip adds to its appeal.

BIRD SONG LISTENING GAME

Learning bird songs and calls is a good way to identify birds—especially those you can't see! Of the nearly 10,000 different bird species in the world, about half of them sing. They are called songbirds. They learn their songs from their parents and neighbors. Their songs are used to attract mates and defend territory. In North America, mostly male songbirds sing. (Female cardinals are one exception . . . and we're learning about more every day!)

Birds also make "calls," which are shorter than songs. Alarm calls signal a threat, such as a predator. Contact calls tell other birds, "Hey, I'm over here!"

Non-songbirds such as phoebes don't have to learn their voices—they're built in. Some birds also make nonvocal sounds. These include the whirring wings of hummingbirds and the drumming of woodpeckers on trees.

Bird soundscapes change throughout the day and over the seasons. Sometimes human-made sounds, such as those from traffic, are so loud they drown out bird sounds. This can prevent bird communication.

ACTIVITY

Sit or stand quietly in a bird-friendly place. Listen for birds for a few minutes. What do you hear? Talk about it. Can anyone identify some of the birds you heard?

Next, for a set period of time, such as two minutes, listen to the birds again. Close your eyes to focus on their sounds. Each time you hear a bird sound, hold up a finger.

How many bird sounds did you hear? Did you recognize any of them? Was there ever a time when it was completely quiet? Were there non-bird sounds, too? What were they?

Now try to find birds that are singing or calling. This can be a challenge. Use your binoculars to see if you can spot an individual bird singing its own special song!

DISCOVERIES

Silent times are rare when birds are around! Listen for the common bird sounds above and see if you can identify what bird is singing.

MATERIALS

+ You just need your ears!

A Tufted Titmouse sings its loud high-pitched song, "*Peter, Peter, Peter!*"

Two Tennessee sisters listen to bird song. One girl looks toward the sound; the other listens intently to "*Fee-bee, Fee-bay!*" It's a Carolina Chickadee!

FOLLOW UP

Get up early and head outside in spring to hear the songbirds' "dawn chorus." Or open windows to catch the free concert. It's worth it!

Recordings, apps, and website videos are good learning tools.

Birds use their **syrinx** to make sounds. Do some research to find out how a bird's syrinx works.

COMMON BIRD SOUNDS

AMERICAN CROW: "*Caw, Caw!*"

AMERICAN GOLDFINCH: "*Potato Chip, Potato Chip!*"

AMERICAN ROBIN: "*Cheer-up, Cheerily, Cheerily!*"

BLUE JAY: "*Jay, Jay!*"

NORTHERN CARDINAL: "*Cheer, Cheer, Cheer! Purty, Purty!*"

TUFTED TITMOUSE: "*Peter, Peter, Peter!*"

Note: You can make up your own words for bird sounds.

BIRD MIGRATION GAME

Many birds fly south each fall to winter sites where they can find food, water, and shelter. They head back north each spring to nest and breed. This annual journey is called **migration**. It can be full of risks, both natural and human-made. By pretending to be migrating birds, players will better understand the hazards birds face during migration and what they need to survive!

This game works best with 10 or more players.

MATERIALS
(FOR 10 OR MORE PLAYERS)

- 50 popsicle sticks (25 green and 25 blue)
- 10 "eggs" (egg-shaped cardboard cut-outs)
- 8 "bird tails" (1' [30 cm]-long ribbons or cloth strips attached to large clips)
- 5 "safe zones" (hula hoops work well)
- 4 corner markers (buckets work well)

OVERVIEW AND PREPARATION

In this game, eight players act as birds running within the flyway from their winter to summer range and back, using safe zones to escape predators (the other two players)! Picking up one egg, two blue sticks, and two green sticks along the way, each player must end up safely in the winter range with tail still on!

To get the game ready, place markers at corners of a large rectangular playing area (about half the size of your school gym works well). Scatter the safe area markers and colored popsicle sticks throughout this area. Scatter eggs at one end of the rectangle behind an imaginary line between markers—this is the summer nesting area. Have eight players line up

Canada Geese fly in a V-formation when migrating. This may help the birds save energy by reducing wind resistance.

Hog Island Audubon campers role play birds migrating to their nesting grounds. The camper on the left gathers food and water while the camper on the right rests in a "safe zone."

behind the opposite line—the winter range. The two predators start in the middle of the migration range. (For a diagram that will help with game setup, see page 58.)

ACTIVITY

BIRDS: Your task is to fly from the winter to summer range and back. Before you fly away, clip a tail onto the back of your shirt.

PREDATORS: You don't get tails, but instead try to pull the tails off the migrating birds. You may not touch birds if they are in a safe zone or in the summer/egg zone. You cannot hover around safe zones, either! (Everyone can have a chance to be a predator in later rounds!)

Birds, you'll have two things to do as you migrate:

1. The popsicle sticks represent food (green) and water (blue). Every bird must pick up one of each color on each part of the migration for a total of four sticks—two green and two blue—to survive the round.

2. The goal of migration is to breed successfully, so you must also pick up one egg from the summer range.

The safe zones are stopover sites (i.e., wetlands, forests, or grasslands) where birds may safely rest with at least one foot within the hoop. If a predator gets a bird's tail, the tail-less bird must wait on the side until the round ends.

(continued)

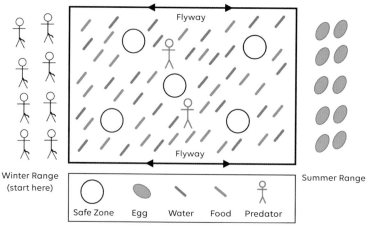

Winter Range (start here)

Summer Range

Safe Zone	Egg	Water	Food	Predator

Birds and predators on your mark. Let the bird migration games begin!

READY, SET, GO!

Play an initial three-minute round to become familiar with the rules. Count down the final ten or twenty seconds out loud—slower birds may not get back in time to survive! For each round, record the number of total birds and the number of survivors.

Have the players replace eggs, re-scatter food and water sticks, and return tails to those who lost them. Pick new predators, play another round, and record the results.

DISCOVERIES

Migration is hard! Bird migration survival is affected by predators and humans. The actions we take can either hinder or help birds on their journey.

FOLLOW UP

Learn more about certain birds' migration journeys. For example, the Arctic Tern migrates from its Arctic nesting sites all the way to Antarctic coastlines and back—a 56,000-mile (90,123 km) round trip that's sometimes even longer! Celebrate World Migratory Bird Day twice a year—on or near the second Saturdays in May and October. Find events or create your own: www.migratorybirdday.org

MIX IT UP

For each round, you may change the game to reflect human impacts upon migration. For example, in round 2, say forests in the summer range have been cut down, so birds will lose nesting sites. Remove some eggs—some birds will not be able to get one! Other possible impacts:

- Wetland filled in: Remove one safe zone.

- Duck hunting: Add a predator.

- New buildings: Remove some food and water sticks.

EASY-TO-MAKE BERRY AND PEANUT BIRD FEEDER LOOP

It's a great feeling watching a bird chow down on a meal you've provided! Simple ingredients such as berries and peanuts can make them happy. After creating a feeder, place it right outside your window so you can see the birds up close. (This will also prevent birds from building up momentum and flying into the glass.)

Carefully pierce and string a berry or two, then a peanut. (Adults should help young children with stringing.) Continue alternating berries and nuts. After you have about a necklace-length, tie the ends of the thread together. Hang your feeder loop from a nearby branch or bird feeder pole. Watch your feathered visitors enjoy your "berry nice" feeder!

ACTIVITY

You can use fresh store-bought berries such as cherries, blueberries, and blackberries, or buy small dried fruits. Or head outside to gather native berries when they're ripe. Birds especially enjoy fall-ripening berries from gray or flowering dogwood, crabapple, and hawthorn trees.

MATERIALS

- Gathered or store-bought berries
- Peanuts in the shell
- Large needle threaded with string or sturdy thread (e.g., nylon)

This bird feeder loop—containing raisins, dried cherries, apricots, cranberries, and peanuts—makes a beautiful and welcome bird treat!

EASY-TO-MAKE BIRD BUTTER PINECONE FEEDER

ACTIVITY

"Bird butter" is a mixture birds can't resist! To make bird butter, combine peanut butter and cornmeal in a large bowl. Mix well. Use a knife to spread some mixture onto pinecones. Tie a string loop to the top of each cone so you can hang it up. Hang the feeders from a nearby tree branch. You can spread any extra bird butter onto the bark of a nearby tree.

DISCOVERIES

It might take a while for your neighborhood birds to find these new treats. Be patient. They'll find them before long. If you feed them, they will come!

FOLLOW UP

If you have a store-bought bird feeder, fill it with seeds birds love, such as black oil sunflower seeds and white proso millet. Put it up and watch your bird visitors enjoy a free meal! Identify and record the birds that visit.

MATERIALS

- 2 cups (500 g) peanut butter
- 1 cup (120 g) cornmeal
- Pinecones (at least one per child)
- Large bowl
- Butter knife
- String

Make the pine cone "bird butter" feeder even more inviting! Roll it in bird seed and colorful dried fruit bits.

PLANTS FOR BIRDS

Want to create a bed-and-breakfast for birds where they can settle down and raise a family? Remember these six words: *More bird-friendly plants, less lawn*! You'll soon have a garden that's alive with birds.

ACTIVITIES

Choose one or all.

GET RID OF GRASS

From a bird's point of view, grass lawns are like deserts. They offer little food or shelter. Perennial plants such as bearberry and creeping juniper are better choices. Unlike lawn grass, these plants provide food and cover for birds—and they don't need mowing! Gas-powered lawnmowers spew millions of tons of carbon dioxide (a greenhouse gas) every year, among other pollutants that negatively impact air quality. Reducing your lawn—and using a human-powered push mower—will shrink your family's carbon footprint.

CREATE LEAF BEDS

Birds such as sparrows scratch for hidden insects under fallen leaves. You can provide them with an ongoing insect supply. In fall, rake a layer of leaves several inches (cm) thick underneath trees and shrubs to create leaf mulch beds. By spring, these leaves will be decomposing into rich soil, providing plenty of earthworms and insects for robins and other ground-feeding birds.

GIMME SHELTER!

Simple brush piles provide good shelter for small birds escaping predators. And they're easy to make! Start with a bed of leaves in a corner of your backyard or schoolyard. Next, add a row of medium-size branches. Then, lay a row of long, thin sticks perpendicular to the branches. Finally, crisscross, adding another row of sticks going in the same direction as the branches. Alternate back and forth, log cabin style, creating as many layers as you can. Keep open spaces within the pile so there's plenty of room for birds. Finish with dry vines and plant clippings on the top and sides.

(continued)

MATERIALS

- Backyard or schoolyard patch of ground
- Rake and trowel for each child
- Native groundcovers / berry-producing saplings to plant

This American Robin is about to gulp down a yummy ripe holly berry.

BETTER FOR BIRDS

"Native" plants have been around for a long, long time. These plants occur naturally in a particular area and have not been introduced by humans. Birds have co-evolved with native plants and are well-adapted to using them for food and shelter. Native plants also require less water and fertilizer than exotic nursery plants, so they're better for the environment.

Many native trees and shrubs have berries that ripen in the fall, just when birds preparing to migrate need to gain weight for their journey. Native flowering dogwood and spicebush produce berries that are high in fat and just the right size for many birds to swallow. These berries turn bright red when they're ripe, signaling "I'm ready to eat!"

Native oaks are like bird grocery stores. Many caterpillars that feed on oak leaves are great food for breeding birds. Long-lived trees such as native oaks and maples also store lots of carbon dioxide. Keeping this greenhouse gas out of the atmosphere helps fight climate change.

To become a better bird gardener, learn to recognize bird-friendly native plants. Water, weed, and protect those that are already there. Then, plant more of them!

DISCOVERIES

Any patch of land can become a more bird-friendly habitat.

FOLLOW UP

Take a look at the yards around you. Which ones have the most birds? Why?

BIRD-ATTRACTING PLANTS

CARDINAL FLOWER (*Lobelia cardinalis*): hummingbirds

CHERRIES (*Prunus* spp.): Cedar Waxwings, thrushes, bluebirds, catbirds, mockingbirds

DOGWOODS (*Cornus* spp.): cardinals, titmice, bluebirds

ELDERBERRIES (*Sambucus* spp.): robins, bluebirds, catbirds, Red-eyed Vireos, Cedar Waxwings

HOLLIES (*Ilex* spp.): catbirds, mockingbirds, cardinals, robins

PENSTEMONS (*Penstemon* spp.): hummingbirds

PINES (*Pinus* spp.): finches, nuthatches

OAKS (*Quercus* spp.): woodpeckers, jays, titmice, chickadees

SALVIAS (*Salvia* spp.): hummingbirds

SERVICEBERRIES (*Amelanchier* spp.): tanagers, grosbeaks, waxwings, robins, orioles, thrushes

SUNFLOWERS/CONEFLOWERS (*Helianthus* spp.) / (*Echinacea* spp.): jays, finches, titmice, grosbeaks, chickadees, nuthatches

Cardinal flower is a great native nectar plant for hummingbirds.

TRUMPET HONEYSUCKLE (*Lonicera sempervirens*): hummingbirds, Purple Finches, Hermit Thrushes, orioles

VIRGINIA CREEPER (*Parthenocissus quinquefolia*): mockingbirds, nuthatches, woodpeckers, jays

Note: spp. is shorthand for species.

SUNFLOWERS FOR SONGBIRDS

Sunflowers—native to North America—have been bred to produce large flowering heads with oily seeds that are especially nutritious for birds. One variety, black oil sunflower seed, is especially popular. Try growing sunflowers yourself and you'll have more birds to watch!

MATERIALS

- Shovel for digging up soil
- Compost
- Trowel for digging seed holes and weeding
- Watering can
- Packets of various sunflower seeds

  NOTE: There are nearly 70 sunflower species in the United States. You'll have lots to choose from!

- Patch of ground in a yard, school, or community garden

ACTIVITY

When spring temperatures hit 70 degrees Fahrenheit (21 degrees Celsius), it's time to dig up the dirt where you want to plant your seeds. Sunflowers grow best in a sunny area! Mix in some compost to enrich the soil. Plant sunflower seeds about 6" (15 cm) apart in a shallow trench about 1" (2.5 cm) deep.

Cover the seeds back up with soil and water daily if there's no rain. Your seeds should sprout in about a week. When the second set of leaves appear, thin your seedlings until they are about 2' (61 cm) apart.

After your sunflowers have bloomed and faded, the flower heads will go to seed. Leave them on the stalks for birds to munch on. Or cover some up with netting to save for winter bird snacks! When netted seed heads are completely dry, cut them off. Store them inside in a cool, dry place, such as a bucket lined with newspaper to absorb moisture. In winter, set the dried seed heads outside as a special bird treat!

DISCOVERIES

Even a few sunflowers can attract birds!

Tip:
You might need support stakes. Sunflowers can grow tall. By fall, your sunflowers may be bigger than you! Have an adult help you if your sunflowers need stakes for support.

Male goldfinch visits a sunflower. Sometimes sunflower seeds spilled from a bird feeder plant themselves—as this one did.

This Hog Island Audubon camper fills a bird feeder with sunflower seeds, millet, and peanuts. Avian attention to follow!

FOLLOW UP

The largest—and perhaps easiest to identify—family of plants is the sunflower. It includes black-eyed Susans, coneflowers, and daisies.

Visit Audubon's Native Plants Database to find the best native plants and trees for your local birds: www.audubon.org/native-plants.

SUNFLOWER SEED BALLS

For extra fun, make sunflower seed balls to plant or give away as gifts! Form small, ping-pong ball–size balls of wet clay mixed with about a teaspoon (1 g) of soil. Tuck a few sunflower seeds inside each ball. Allow to dry until hard. Then give away or plant your seed balls. Water, weed, and wait!

HUMMINGBIRD HAVENS

Bird artist John James Audubon called hummingbirds "glittering fragments of the rainbow." Many are named for their gem-like appearance—including Ruby-throated and Emerald-chinned hummingbirds. Twelve hummingbird species regularly breed in the United States. Want to attract hummers? Plant nectar-filled flowers for these long-distance fliers to fuel up on before migration, or to provide energy for their daily "bug" hunts. Enjoy watching them flit from flower to flower!

Bright-red, orange, and pink perennial flowers are hummingbird magnets! If flowers are tube-shaped, even better. Tubular flowers store nectar at the bottom, which encourages these long-beaked little birds to probe for a sweet meal. In the process, pollen sticks to the hummer's head to pollinate nearby flowers.

MATERIALS

- Seed packets or starter plants of hummer-attracting native perennials (e.g., bee balm, columbine, cardinal flower, red salvia, and pineapple sage)

- Trowel for digging holes

- Potting soil

- Pots or planters of various sizes

TIP: Unglazed clay pots allow air and moisture to move in and out—that's good for plants, but they're breakable. Any sort of clean container can grow plants: baskets, buckets, even old wooden bird houses. The key is drainage. All pots need drainage holes. Plant roots left in water can rot!

Cool!
These tiniest of vertebrates, relative to their body size, have the largest brain, fastest wing beat, quickest heartbeat, highest body temperature, and greatest appetite of any bird!

A female Ruby-throated Hummingbird visits salvia flowers. The nectar will help her put on weight before migrating south for the winter.

The male Ruby-throated Hummingbird's throat patch (gorget) sparkles when the sun hits it just right! Here a male sips sugar-water nectar.

ACTIVITY

Plant a couple of seeds or single seedlings in individual pots. Follow directions on seed packets to learn how deep to plant your seeds.

Alternately, plant three to five different flowering plants in one large pot to create a big hummingbird container garden. Plant the largest-growing plants in the center of a multi-plant pot.

If you're starting with young plants: Fill two-thirds of your pot or pots with lightweight potting soil mix. Gently place the plants in the soil. Be careful with the roots. Remember, healthy roots equal healthy plants. Finally, add a bit more soil and water well!

Once your flowers bloom, watch these mini birds enjoy their hummer haven!

DISCOVERIES

Even a few plant pots full of colorful flowers can attract hummingbirds. Who else is visiting your flowers?

FOLLOW UP

Put up hummingbird sugar-water feeders. A recipe of four parts water (1 cup, or 235 ml) to one part white cane sugar (¼ cup, or 50 g) is most like flower nectar.

3 INSIDE WITH THE BIRDS:

GAMES, ACTIVITIES, AND ADVENTURES

Don't let a rainy day get you down! Fun and discovery await you inside, with bird-related activities that can be done at home, in any classroom, or in a nature center.

Get ready for your next birdwatching adventure by sharpening up your bird identification skills using field guides and apps. Then learn about the field marks that all birders use in the field. Discover how popular birds are by looking for bird images in your home or school—and finding them everywhere! And see how big birds really are by studying their wingspans. (They're longer than you might think!)

In this chapter, we'll also offer some easy ways to help our feathered friends. With a few tools and a bit of adult help, you can build a simple nesting shelf for your local robins and House Finches ... and an even simpler nest basket for Mourning Doves. Find out which foods attract which birds and learn how birds use their beaks to eat their food.

The activities in this chapter are just a sample of the many ways to learn about birds indoors. We hope you enjoy them!

KID HERO: OLIVIA BOULER

Young artist Olivia Bouler, saddened by the 2010 Gulf Coast oil spill, wrote a letter to Audubon, which she signed "11 years old and willing to help." She offered to send one of her original bird paintings to everyone who donated to the oil-damaged birds' recovery. The idea took flight! Bouler created and sent out more than 500 paintings, helping to raise more than $200,000 to help the birds. She later wrote and illustrated a book called *Olivia's Birds: Saving the Gulf*. Bouler continues to speak out for birds to this day.

◄◄ It's fun to get up close and personal with a Black-capped Chickadee! This Illinois elementary school student is watching birds for the Great Backyard Bird Count.

HOW TO GO BIRDING INDOORS

Indoor days are perfect for sharpening your bird ID skills—using both sight and sound. You can also review bird lists, write in your bird journal, and practice community science bird counts. Get busy indoor birding!

ACTIVITY

Chapter 1 of this book provides a good start for learning the common birds around you—along with fun facts and bird jokes! But don't stop there. Field guides are packed with bird info: Try Audubon, Peterson, Sibley, or National Geographic to start. There are also the Crossley Bird ID guides and *The Young Birder's Guide to Birds of North America*.

Free apps and websites can turn your phone into a pocket field guide. Many have audio clips of songs and calls. Some also have ways to create electronic lists of all the birds you see and hear!

Check out these apps:

- Audubon Bird Guide app: Explore U.S. birds. Built for all ages.
- Merlin ID app: More than 1,100 North American species.
- eBird app: Displays birding hotspots and real-time sightings.

Visit these websites:

- All About Birds online (Cornell Lab of Ornithology): www.allaboutbirds.org
- Audubon Guide to North American Birds (Audubon): www.audubon.org/bird-guide

DISCOVERIES

Indoor birding has its advantages, including not getting wet or cold!

MATERIALS

- Field guides (books, apps, or online)
- Computer or smartphone
- Journal
- Writing and art supplies

A homeschooler sketches a Wood Thrush from a photo on her computer.

FOLLOW UP

These community science projects will carry you through the seasons:

- Christmas Bird Count: Join the nation's oldest bird count (National Audubon Society).

- Project FeederWatch: Watch birds at feeders for science (Cornell Lab of Ornithology).

- Great Backyard Bird Count: Find global bird reports in real time (eBird).

- Hummingbirds at Home: Watch hummers! Report on flowers they visit (National Audubon Society).

BIRD JOURNALING

Try starting a bird journal! Add bird observations, photos, and drawings from your recent bird walks and birdwatching.

BIRD CLUES:
The Six S Questions

Learn general bird identification clues and field marks before going outside to watch fast, flitting birds! Beginning birders can use six questions that start with S as a great aid to bird identification.

- **SIZE**: How big is the bird? Is it about the size of a sparrow, robin, crow, or larger?
- **SHAPE**: What is the bird's overall shape? Is it thin or rounded? Plump or sleek?
- **SHADE**: What colors are on the bird? Where on the bird's body are these colors found?
- **SURROUNDINGS**: What habitat is this bird found in?
- **SWEEP**: Does this bird have any notable flight characteristics?
- **SONG**: What songs, calls, or other sounds does this bird make? Try to imitate it!

Field marks are birds' unique spots, stripes, feather colors, and patterns that help birders—and maybe even the birds themselves—recognize different species and individuals. Look for field marks on the head and wings. Check out the beak shape and color. Does the bird have an eyebrow stripe or a throat patch? Are there any stripes on the wings (wingbars)?

MATERIALS
(FOR ANY SIZE GROUP, WORKING IN PAIRS)

- A partner
- This book and/or other field guides
- A smartphone, tablet, or computer
- Notebook and pens or pencils

ACTIVITY

Select a common bird profiled in this book. Have your partner do the same, and don't tell your partner which bird you picked! Using a field guide, this book, and/or a computer if needed, research and write down the answers to the six S questions for your chosen bird. Be sure to include some distinctive field marks.

Now try to guess each other's bird! Taking turns, each player should begin by describing one of the six "S's" on the selected bird—then continue, one S at a time. See how fast the other player can guess your bird.

WHO AM I?

I'm a Carolina Wren! Who are you?

SIZE: sparrow-sized

SHAPE: stout, round

SHADE: reddish-brown above, buffy below

SURROUNDINGS: wooded areas

SWEEP: rapid flight

SONG: *"Teakettle, Teakettle!"*

FIELD MARK: white eyebrow

DISCOVERY

Which of the S words gives the bird away quickest? Notice that no two bird species has the same six S answers!

FOLLOW UP

Head outside and find an unfamiliar bird. Answer as many of the six S questions as you can about this live, wild bird. Try to identify the bird based on your observations, including specific field marks.

BIRDS ARE EVERYWHERE!

Many people collect bird art and bird stamps. But once you start looking, you'll also notice bird images on clothing, curtains, mugs, and more. See how many you can find! Then try to identify some of the birds.

ACTIVITY

Go on an indoor scavenger hunt! Try to find the following:

1. Bird image on clothing

2. Bird photo or drawing in a book, magazine, or newspaper

3. Bird photo or drawing hung on a wall

4. Bird image on a plate or mug

5. Bird stuffie or another toy

6. Bird image somewhere you didn't expect it!

DISCOVERIES

Check your potholders, refrigerator magnets, calendars, and T-shirts! Bird images are "hidden in plain sight" everywhere. (Especially cardinals!)

FOLLOW UP

Birds can be right on the money! Some countries put images of their native birds on coins or cash. On the back of the U.S. $1 bill, you'll find the national emblem: the Bald Eagle (below, right). And the Common Loon is featured on Canada's dollar coin (below, left)—appropriately called a *loonie*! Look for other birds on U.S. and foreign currency. Learn why these birds were chosen to be honored.

BIRD BODIES:
What's on a Bird?

Once you know your bird body parts, you'll be better able to identify birds and share your bird sightings with others. Most birds have the same essential body parts, so get to know the topography! *Note: Many bird guides have bird topography sections.*

The body parts of a Black-capped Chickadee

MATERIALS

* Paper or tracing paper
* Coloring supplies such as crayons, markers, or colored pencils

ACTIVITY

Either draw a bird or create an outline by tracing over a photo of a bird. Birds come in many shapes and sizes, but you should still be able to identify the following parts (working clockwise):

* Crown (top of head)
* Beak
* Throat
* Breast
* Belly
* Feet
* Rump
* Wing
* Back
* Nape (back of neck)

Label and color in each body part. Be creative in your color choices!

DISCOVERIES

Many bird body parts are similar to human body parts, although some are different.

FOLLOW UP

Choose a land bird to learn about. Study that bird's features, using field guides or online photos. Then trace an outline of the bird and color it accordingly. Repeat using an outline of a water bird (e.g., a duck).

HOW WIDE IS YOUR WINGSPAN?

Bird wingspans vary a lot. On average, a Ruby-throated Hummingbird's wingspan is about 4½" (11 cm). On the other hand, a California Condor's is about 10' (3.1 m). The wingspan record goes to an extinct bird (*Pelagornis sandersi*)—about 22' (6.7 m)!

ACTIVITY

Look up a small bird's wingspan (often abbreviated as WS) in a field guide or online. Write it down. For example, a House Finch's WS is 9.5" (24 cm). *Note: Measurements are averages.*

Measure your bird's WS out on paper (placing the long side toward you). Mark it, then cut the paper to that length. Fold the paper in half, wingtip to wingtip, pinch the fold, and try giving those wings a flap!

Tip: Wing width can be eyeballed. A 3" (8 cm) width works well for small birds. Double that (or go even wider, if necessary) for large birds.

MATERIALS

- Scissors
- Measuring tape
- Masking tape
- Rubber bands to fit over arm or wrist (two per child)
- Scrap 8½" × 11" (22 cm x 28 cm) A4 or other standard-sized paper paper (smaller paper can be used for smaller birds)
- Long pieces of cardboard or packing paper
- Field guides

The Great Black-backed Gull's average wingspan measures nearly 5½ feet (168 cm)!

An environmental educator at the Audubon Center in Greenwich, Connecticut, spreads his "wings" over young birders.

Now look up a larger bird. A Herring Gull's WS, for example, is 58"—nearly 5' (1.5 m)! Gather long pieces of cardboard or paper, or tape pieces together. Mark and cut to the length needed for the big set of wings.

Fold your new wings in half length-wise. Have someone place the fold on your back, just below your neck. You can tape or secure the wings to clothing on both sides of the fold. For longer wings, try taping wingtips to your sleeves, or put a rubber band loosely around your wings to hold them in place. Flap those wings!

DISCOVERIES

Wingspans, especially for big birds such as Herring and Great Black-backed gulls, are longer than you might think!

FOLLOW UP

Stretch out your arms as wide as you can. Have someone measure your "wingspan" from longest finger to longest finger. What bird is closest to your own wingspan?

Fun Fact:
Your wingspan is about the same as your height!

THE MANY TYPES OF FEATHERS

Bird feathers come in many different types. Flight feathers in the wings and tail are for lifting off the Earth and flying. Bristle feathers, found around many birds' face and eyes, are sharp and stiff like cat whiskers. They block dirt and dust, control squirming insect prey, and help birds sense their surroundings. Down feathers keep birds warm and dry.

Flight feather from a Red-shouldered Hawk

Down feather

Bristle feather

WHAT MAKES A GOOD BIRDHOUSE?

By the mid-1900s, bluebird populations had gone way down. Good birdhouses helped restore their numbers. But bluebirds still need nest boxes today. Other cavity-nesting birds, including chickadees, swallows, and wrens, also benefit from well-designed birdhouses. Consider putting up your own! Use the guide below to buy a birdhouse.

ACTIVITY

Explore the nest boxes in your neighborhood or in local garden, hardware, and bird stores that stock birdhouses. Which are good birdhouses? Which are bad? Here's what to look for:

BIRDHOUSES TO AVOID

- Heavily painted nest boxes. Paint can be toxic. Dark colors can create oven-like conditions.
- Perches on birdhouses. Perches give predators easy access to the eggs and chicks inside!
- Wrong-size entry holes. Holes that are too large allow predators inside. Learn what size hole is best for the birds you want to attract.
- Poor construction. Avoid stapled-together birdhouses made from flimsy materials. They'll soon fall apart.

This birdhouse is a decoration, not a bird home. It can't be opened to clean it. Entry hole perches invite predators, stapled connections are flimsy, and pointed roofs are prone to leak.

This easy-to-open, easy-to-clean, well-ventilated nest box was home to two broods of Eastern Bluebirds—ten chicks—in 2019!

BIRDHOUSES TO USE

- Houses made of unpainted wood (cedar, cypress, or pine boards at least ¾" [2 cm] thick). These are most like a cavity-nesting bird's natural home.

- Houses with ventilation holes. Holes allow moisture and heat to escape.

- Houses with an overhanging roof. 2" (5 cm) of overhang in front and 1" (2.5 cm) on the sides, will help block rain and provide shade.

- Houses that are easy to access and clean. Can you open the nest box easily? A front opening that hinges at the bottom is a good design.

DISCOVERIES

Often the most bedazzling birdhouses are the most dangerous for birds! Use them for decorations instead.

FOLLOW UP

Clean out your birdhouse in early spring, before birds return, and if time permits, again in late fall after the birds have left.

EASY-TO-MAKE MOURNING DOVE NEST BASKET

Your local Mourning Doves will be delighted to find this cozy nest basket! Hopefully they'll use it to raise a family. Adult help and supervision are required for this project.

ACTIVITY

Create a simple Mourning Dove nest basket by following these steps:

1. Cut the screen square into a 12" (30 cm) circle. Trim off any sharp wires that may be sticking out.

2. Cut out a piece of the pie—a small pie-shaped slice about 2½" (6 cm) wide on the outer edge of the circle.

3. Pull the edges of the remaining circle together to form a cone.

4. "Sew" the edges together with wire. Make sure no sharp wires remain.

5. Place the cone, basket side up, in the fork of a tree branch at least 5' (1.5 m) off the ground. Conifer trees are ideal.

6. Use remaining wire to attach the nest basket securely to the branch in several places.

DISCOVERIES

A Mourning Dove pair may fill your nest basket with a loose nest made of sticks and pine needles. The male gathers materials while the female weaves the nest.

Each season, the Mourning Dove parents may raise three families—or even more—in your nest basket! Each family, or brood, begins life as two white eggs. The parents take turns sitting on the eggs for two weeks—the male by day and the female at night. When the chicks hatch, parents feed them for another two weeks until they are ready to fledge (fly away).

MATERIALS

- 12" × 12" (30 cm × 30 cm) square of ¼" (6 mm) mesh metal screening (hardware cloth)

- Small length of wire, about 16" (41 cm) long

- Tin snips for cutting

FOLLOW UP

You can help Mourning Doves even more by keeping your cat inside, providing birdseed in a platform (tray) feeder, or simply scattering the birdseed on the ground.

An evergreen tree is a great place for your Mourning Dove nest basket. Wire the basket securely to the branch in several places.

1. With a pair of tin snips, cut a 12" × 12" (30 x 30 cm) piece of galvanized hardware cloth.

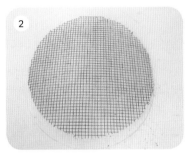

2. Cut a 12" (30 cm) diameter circle out of the piece. Trim off any sharp edges.

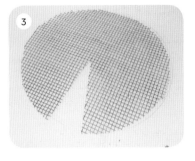

3. Cut out a "piece of pie"—2½ inches (6 cm) wide at the "crust" side.

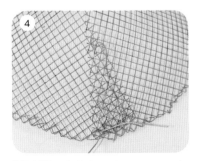

4. Fold the circle to make a cone, and "sew" it together with a wire at the seam. Fold under the circle edges to create smooth edges.

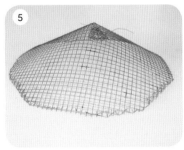

5. Fold the top of the cone over so no sharp edges face the nest basket area.

EASY-TO-MAKE NESTING SHELF FOR ROBINS AND HOUSE FINCHES

Birds need places to nest! Instead of an Elf on the Shelf, you can have robins, House Finches, or other birds on a shelf! They may use your handy, simple L-shaped nesting shelf to raise a family. Speaking of family—this is a great project to make with a parent! Adult help and supervision are required for this project, especially for the drilling.

MATERIALS

- 1" × 6" × 12¾" (3 × 15 × 32 cm) pine, cedar, or cypress board, cut into two pieces: a 6" × 6¾" (15 × 17 cm) longer back piece and a 6" × 6" (15 × 15 cm) shorter shelf piece

  NOTE: Lumber stores may pre-cut boards to the smaller pieces you need to make the nesting shelf.

- 4 exterior-grade deck screws to attach the two pieces together

- 2 screws to hang the shelf

ACTIVITY

Create a simple nesting shelf by following these steps:

1. Make 2 holes at the top (6" [15 cm]) end of the longer back piece for attaching to a wall later.

2. Pre-drill 4 holes into the 1" (3 cm)–thick bottom of this same back piece. Pre-drilling will help you avoid splitting the wood!

3. Attach the shelf (floor) piece to the back piece, using the 4 screws.

4. Hang the shelf on a wall in a sheltered location with an overhang or ceiling (e.g., a porch), using 2 screws that fit through the holes. Leave a robin's worth of space (8" [20 cm] or so) between the shelf and the ceiling. See who visits—and who stays!

DISCOVERIES

A robin may build her mud-and-twig nest on your shelf, lay 3 to 5 sky blue eggs, and raise three broods per season! A female House Finch might build a grass nest and lay 4 to 5 spotted gray-green eggs. Enjoy watching the eggs hatch and the chicks fledge!

FOLLOW UP

Handy persons, consider going further! To offer birds more cover and security, you can add a roof and sides to the shelf.

A female robin built this nest using her feet and bill to shape the mud and twigs. Then she lined the nest with soft grasses.

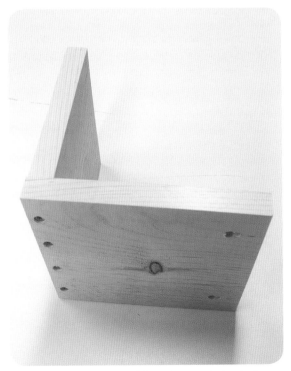

Four screws attach the shelf floor piece to the back piece. Two pre-drilled screw holes at the top of the piece are for adhering to a wall.

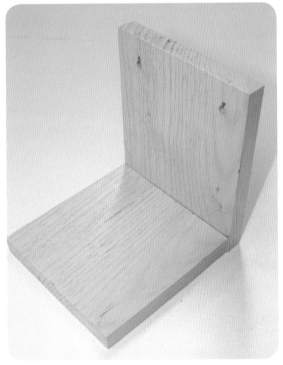

Time to hang up your nesting shelf and hope birds choose it for their home!

BIRD FEEDING EXPERIMENT

Do you enjoy watching birds visit feeders? Would you like to know what foods they like best? Pick out four different kinds of bird food commonly sold in garden and hardware stores. Come up with a hypothesis (an educated guess) about which food will be the most popular with backyard birds. Then do the following activity to find out if your hypothesis is correct!

ACTIVITY

Fill each of the four pans with a different bird food. Set them outside on the ground in a row. Put them where you can see them from an inside window—preferably near an existing bird feeder.

MATERIALS

- 4 identical aluminum pie pans
- 4 kinds of bird food (e.g., black oil sunflower seeds, millet, peanuts, and cracked corn)
- Paper for data sheets
- Pencil

SAMPLE DATA SHEET   Observation Day #1__ #2__ #3__ (check one)

Collect data for 15 minutes. Make a hash mark for each bird visit. Identify the bird if you know it. After 15 minutes, add up the number of visits, as shown below.

Date_____ Time_____ Weather _____ (fill in)

1) Peanuts	2) Sunflower	3) Millet	4) Corn
Non ID'd: I (1)	IIII I (6)		I (1)
ID'd : Blue Jay III (3)	Chickadee IIII (4)		
TOTAL VISITS	TOTAL VISITS	TOTAL VISITS	TOTAL VISITS
4	10	0	1

Notes: Write down bird behaviors you observe, such as squabbles, birds that fly away with food, birds that stay at pans and eat, odd-looking birds, non-bird visitors (e.g., squirrels).

Lucky are the birds who'll taste-test these pie pan treats. From left to right: peanuts, black-oil sunflower seed, millet and cracked corn.

Come back inside. Make a simple data sheet with four columns for the four foods you are offering. For example, title the first column: "1: Peanuts" (if peanuts are in the left pan). Title the next column "2: Sunflower Seeds" (if sunflower seeds are in the next pan), and so on. Now record the date, time, and weather at the top of the page. Set a timer for 15 minutes and get comfy!

Whenever you see a bird eat from a pan, write it down in the appropriate column. (Identify the bird if you can.) After 15 minutes, bring the pans back in.

You've got data! Check your results. Which food was most popular? Which birds preferred which foods? If no birds ate your food, that's okay. "Null" data are still data! A longer observation time will likely produce more data.

Repeat the experiment at the same time on Day #2. Record your results on a new data sheet. Did you get the same results? Repeat on Day #3. Compare your results.

Note: Ground-feeding birds such as doves and sparrows—and maybe other critters such as squirrels—might be your best customers!

DISCOVERIES

Different birds prefer different foods! Some foods attract more kinds of birds than others.

Colorful cardinals may visit your pie pans!

FOLLOW UP

Might the time of day, the weather, or the location of the food be a factor? See what happens if you offer food in the morning versus the evening, or on a sunny day compared to a rainy day, or with the pan positions switched. Come up with your own experiments!

BIRD BEAK ADAPTATIONS:
Which Beak for Which Food?

As you have probably noticed, birds have no teeth! So, bird food is not chewed—it's ground up in the **gizzard**. Bird beaks, or bills, are still important for eating, though. Birds use them to pick up food, crack seeds, or stab prey. Bird beaks vary in size and shape. Different beaks work best for different foods. In this activity, you'll use a variety of objects to mimic different bird beaks and different bird foods.

ACTIVITY

Fill each aluminum tray with one of these "foods:"

1. Soil with strings (representing earthworms) both on top of and underneath 1" (2.5 cm) of soil

2. Cork pieces (representing pond plants) floating on 1" (2.5 cm) of water

3. Sunflower seeds

For the fourth food, fill the tall glass with water (representing flower nectar). Each team receives one of the above types of wild bird food and tools that mimic bird beaks: tweezers (robin's beak), pliers (cardinal's beak), a small net (duck's bill), and an eyedropper (hummingbird's beak).

Each player tries using each tool (beak) for a timed 10-second period to pick up as much food as possible. Place the picked up (eaten) food into a large measuring cup. Record the amount, then dump it back for the next player.

MATERIALS

- Timer
- Field guides, posters, or projected images of robins, cardinals, ducks, and hummingbirds

FOR EACH TEAM OF 2–5 PLAYERS:
- 3 rectangular, recyclable 2" (5 cm)–deep aluminum trays
- Bag of potting soil
- 25 pieces of string, each about 2" (5 cm)
- Handful of small corks or cork pieces (crumbled wine corks work fine!)
- Bag of sunflower seeds for bird feeders
- Tall glass
- Pitcher of water
- Large measuring cup
- Tweezers
- Pliers
- Small net
- Eyedropper

Which "beak" can pick up these yummy white pipe cleaner worms? From left to right: net, pliers, eye dropper, and tweezers.

American Robin

Repeat using the next tool until each player has tried out each of the four beaks on that food. Then it's time to try a different type of bird food and repeat the process. Make sure everyone gets to try all four bird beaks on all four foods.

DISCOVERIES

Which bird beak tool worked best for:

- Robins to gobble up string worms? *Tweezers!*
- Cardinals to grab sunflower seeds? *Pliers!*
- Ducks to scoop up pond plants? *Net!*
- Hummingbirds to sip flower nectar? *Eye dropper!*

FOLLOW UP

Look at close-up photos of robins, cardinals, ducks, and hummingbirds. Notice the length and shape of each bird's beak. Can the beak help you guess each bird's habitat? (Hint: What natural foods might be found within that habitat?) What might happen to a bird if the food it needs is not there? Do you think different species of birds can feed side by side without competing for food? What else are bird beaks used for (e.g., building nests, courting mates, and preening feathers)?

Male and female Mallards

Male Northern Cardinal

A male Ruby-throated Hummingbird sticks out its tongue!

APPENDIX
Learn More & Get Involved!

In the late 1800s and early 1900s, U.S. birds suffered from overhunting. Massive numbers were killed simply for their feathers, which were mostly used to decorate women's hats. Birds such as the Great Egret nearly went extinct. Long breeding plumes from the back of this beautiful white wading bird were highly prized.

Outraged by the slaughter, early Audubon groups worked for better laws. The result? The 1918 Migratory Bird Treaty Act. This law, which banned the killing of migratory birds, has since saved billions of birds, including entire species.

Great Egret populations bounced back after the law was passed. Today this bird is a conservation success story and it's the symbol of the National Audubon Society.

Wild birds still need our help today. Living with humans is a challenge for them in many ways. A 2019 study in the journal *Science* found great losses even among common birds like blackbirds, finches, sparrows, and swallows over the past 50 years. The study raises concerns about the health of bird populations. In the pages that follow, you'll find some ways we can work together to make our modern world more bird-friendly.

REDUCING BIRD DANGERS

CLIMATE CHANGE

Greenhouse gases are building up in the Earth's atmosphere. They are making the Earth warmer.

A warmer planet affects birds by changing their habitats, food sources, and migration. Help birds out by learning more about climate change and sharing this knowledge with your friends, parents, and teachers. You'll find there are many things you can do, such as recycling and using less plastic. You can also help birds deal with climate change by planting bird-friendly plants (see page 63).

LEAD-POISONED BIRDS

As many as 3 million U.S. birds die from lead poisoning each year. This happens when loons ingest lead fishing weights, for example, or raptors feed on the remains of a deer killed with a lead bullet. Lead-poisoned birds become too weak to fly or feed themselves. A single bullet fragment can kill a Bald Eagle! You can help:

◆ Promote nontoxic ammunition (e.g., copper bullets) and non-lead fishing tackle.

This Red-tailed Hawk had fed on a deer carcass containing lead bullet shards. Nicknamed Ledbelly, he required months of rehabilitation for lead poisoning at Cornell's Swanson Wildlife Health Center in Ithaca, New York.

- Write letters to lawmakers supporting the phasing out of lead products.
- Donate to wildlife hospitals where lead-poisoned animals receive treatment.

PLASTIC TRASH

Think about plastic items we often use once and then throw away: cups, straws, utensils, grocery bags, and more. Like all plastics, single-use plastic lasts for centuries in the environment. Most ends up in the ocean. Meanwhile, discarded six-pack rings and fishing line can strangle birds. And eating plastic bits can starve or hurt them. You can help:

- Reduce, reuse, recycle, or refuse single-use plastics whenever you can.
- Use cloth grocery bags, reusable water bottles, and metal mugs and utensils.
- Never release balloons outdoors.
- Tell others about the dangers of plastics; and participate in beach and roadside clean-ups.

WINDOW STRIKES

Millions of birds die every year from crashing into windows. They can't tell the difference between reflected sky and real sky. Screened windows are safest—birds bounce off! Bird feeders should be placed either less than 3' (1 m) or more than 30' (9 m) away from windows. Another remedy: Apply tempera paint or non-transparent tape in vertical stripes to outside window surfaces (⅛" [3 mm] wide, and less than 4" [10 cm] apart). For bird tape and other solutions, visit abcbirds.org/get-involved/bird-smart-glass.

LIGHTS OUT

Most birds migrate by night, using the moon and stars to navigate. Flying over bright city lights confuses them. An estimated billion migrating birds die each year from crashing into buildings. "Lights Out" programs ask building managers to turn off unnecessary lights during migration, saving birds—and energy costs, too. Visit www.audubon.org/conservation/project/lights-out.

CATS INDOORS!

Outdoor cats kill an estimated 2.4 billion—or one in ten—native U.S. birds each year. Nesting and migratory birds are most at risk. Bird groups and humane societies alike recommend keeping cats indoors, both for the birds' safety and the cats' well-being. Indoor cats avoid harmful outdoor threats such as fleas, ticks, rabies, cat fights, poisonous chemicals, aggressive dogs and other predators, and especially cars. If you give your cats toys, catnip, places to climb and scratch, clean litter boxes, and lots of attention, they can live long, happy lives indoors.

But if your cat is as eager to go out as you are to keep her in, an outdoor enclosure, or "catio," can be a good compromise. An enclosure can be as simple as a screened-in porch. Add tree branches, ladders, hanging toys, perching ledges, boxes to hide in, and a tarp over the roof for sun and rain protection. There cats can safely watch squirrels, sleep in the sun, and stalk bugs that make the mistake of wandering in! Easy-to-build cat enclosure kits are available from places such as C & D Pet Products (www.cdpets.com) and Cats on Deck (www.catsondeck.com).

Cats live longer, safer lives indoors...and the birds are safer too!

HELPING INJURED BIRDS

1. Ask an adult for help before approaching an injured bird.

2. Prepare a rescue box. Punch some air holes on top and line it with a blanket or towel. Have another towel or cloth ready. Even a jacket will do!

3. Put on gloves if available. Approach the bird slowly and quietly. If the bird remains still, it may be sick, injured, or stunned from hitting a window. Or it may be a fledgling too young to fly—if so, leave it alone (see #6).

   Another person in front of an injured bird can help distract it. Approaching from the rear, put the towel over the bird. Keeping the wings folded against the bird's body, gently lift it up and place it in the lined box. Remove the covering towel. Put it over the closed box to block the light.

4. If you suspect a window strike, place the boxed bird in a warm, dark, quiet place to recover. If you hear movement within an hour or two, the stunned bird may be ready to fly. Open the box outside and say goodbye! If the bird still cannot fly, see #5.

5. For more serious injuries, call a local bird rehabilitator, wildlife clinic, or veterinarian. Find out if they will accept the bird. If so, have an adult transport the boxed bird. Meanwhile, don't try to make an injured bird eat or drink water. A weak bird could drown or get wet and chilled.

6. Grounded fledglings may be fine. Many try to fly before their wings are strong enough. They plop to the ground, where they may spend several days. Their parents are likely close by and still feeding them. Simply keep dogs and cats away. Don't be a bird-napper!

7. Newly hatched, featherless chicks also sometimes fall from nests. If you can't find the nest, chicks may have a better chance of survival with a wildlife rehabilitator. But if you can see and reach the nest, gently put these chicks back. Will parent birds reject them if they smell a human? Nope. That's a myth!

Look at this bird! Look at *that* bird! Seeing birds up close—and birding back-to-back—is fun!

LEARN MORE:
NATURE CENTERS, BIRD CLUBS, AND FESTIVALS

Want to learn more about birds from ornithology experts and other young birders? Explore the possibilities below. Although most bird camps are for teens or adults, younger birders have plenty of bird-learning opportunities. Some involve family members of all ages.

NATURE CENTERS offer bird walks, classes, and sometimes summer youth camps where you can meet local birds and birders. The National Audubon Society runs more than 40 centers nationwide.

BIRD CLUBS connect birders young and old and take field trips near and far. Most communities have a bird club or Audubon chapter. Join one! Audubon has more than 450 local chapters nationwide.

YOUNG BIRDER CLUBS sometimes form within local bird clubs, Audubon chapters, and state birding associations. Age limits vary. Find the nearest club via the American Birding Association: www.aba.org/connect-with-other-young-birders. None near you? Contact a bird group that may help you start one!

BIRDING FESTIVALS are often designed around bird species, birding events, and weather! Audubon New Jersey's Fall Festival at Cape May is the oldest such event. Another is the Space Coast Birding and Wildlife Festival in Florida, held each January. *Bird Watcher's Digest* magazine has a festival finder: www.birdwatchersdigest.com/bwdsite/explore/festivals. Or create your own birding festival!

BIRD HERO: DREW LANHAM

Drew Lanham first noticed birds as a boy growing up on his family's ranch in rural South Carolina. Despite the prejudice he sometimes encountered as a black birder, birds became his companions and guides to his future path. Today, Lanham is an author, wildlife professor at Clemson University, and birding instructor at the Hog Island Audubon Camp. He shares his love of birds and wilderness with a focus on encouraging more people of color to appreciate the outdoors. Says Lanham, "Coloring the conservation conversation is my mantra!"

GLOSSARY
Words for Birds

ADAPTATION: A change in a bird's behavior or body that has improved its ability to survive.

BIRD ID: Shorthand for "bird identification," commonly used by birders.

BROOD: Group of chicks hatched in same nest; (verb) to sit on eggs.

CACHE: Hidden food; (verb) hiding food to eat later.

CONIFER: Tree or shrub with cones, usually an evergreen.

CONSERVATION: Care and protection of wildlife and its natural habitats.

COURTSHIP: Behavior (i.e., song or movement) displayed to win a mate.

DABBLE: Feeding behavior (dipping head into water, tipping tail up) used by some water birds.

DECIDUOUS: Tree or shrub with leaves that drop each fall.

ENDANGERED: Rare plant, bird, or animal that may soon become extinct.

EXTINCT: Plant, bird, or animal that no longer exists.

FLEDGLING: Young bird nearly or just ready to fly.

FORAGE: To search for food; (noun) bulky food.

GIZZARD: Muscular part of a bird's stomach that grinds up food with grit.

HABITAT: Place where a bird or animal lives and finds the resources it needs.

MIGRATION: Traveling to another location when seasons change to find food and breed.

MULCH: Natural soil cover (i.e., leaves, straw) that controls weeds, holds moisture, and adds nutrients.

OMNIVORE: Bird or animal that eats meat as well as plants.

ORNITHOLOGY: The study of birds.

PERENNIAL: Plant that lives longer than one year and regrows each spring.

PESTICIDE: Insect poison, often harmful to birds that eat the poisoned insects.

PISHING: "Psssh" sound made by birders to attract birds for viewing.

PREDATOR: Bird or animal that lives by killing and eating other animals.

PREENING: Using the beak to straighten and clean feathers.

RESTORATION: Actively returning a habitat to its former, more natural condition.

SCAVENGER: Bird or animal that feeds on dead and decaying animals.

SUET: Wild bird food that contains fat (originally beef kidney fat).

SUSTAINABLE: Use of natural resources in a way that lets them regrow so future generations may continue using them.

SYRINX: A bird's vocal organ, located at the base of its windpipe. (Our human voice box, or larynx, is located at the top of the windpipe, the trachea.)

TERRITORY: Area (i.e., nest site) that a bird or animal defends from others.

VERTEBRATE: Animal with a backbone, including every bird.

WINGSPAN: Distance between a bird's outstretched wingtips.

ABOUT THE AUTHORS

ELISSA WOLFSON has written and edited numerous environmental, botanical, ornithological, and veterinary publications. After graduating from Cornell University, she worked as an environmental educator for a decade, earned an M.S. degree, and transitioned into environmental journalism. Her clients include the National Audubon Society and Cornell University's Laboratory of Ornithology and College of Veterinary Medicine. She is former editor of *E, The Environmental Magazine*, and *Cornell Plantations Magazine*, current editor of *Rationality and Society*, author of *101 Cool Games for Cool Cats* (Rockwell House, 2007), and co-author of the *Audubon Birdhouse Book* (Voyageur Press, 2013) and the *American Museum of Natural History Pocket Birds of North America, Eastern and Western Regions* (DK, 2017).

MARGARET A. BARKER, a Chesapeake Bay–area writer and educator, grew up watching feeder birds in East Tennessee thanks to her bird-loving mother and grandmother. Covering environmental stories during a broadcast journalism career in the southeast, including at WGST, Atlanta, led to an M.S. degree via the Audubon Expedition Institute and an internship with Audubon's Washington, D.C. office. She managed the Cornell Lab of Ornithology's Project FeederWatch and later the Kids Growing Food school garden program for Cornell's Department of Education. She writes for newspapers and magazines, and she is co-author of *The FeederWatcher's Guide to Bird Feeding* (HarperCollins, 2000), the *Audubon Birdhouse Book* (Voyageur Press, 2013), and *Feeding Wild Birds in America* (Texas A&M University Press, 2015).

ACKNOWLEDGMENTS

We thank the Hog Island Audubon Camp instructors and bird educators everywhere who provided ideas and suggested activities to open up the world of birds, both to grownups and to the children in their lives. We also are indebted to bird photographers. May your perfect images inspire readers to pursue their own birding adventures. And to the teachers in our lives who shared their love and knowledge of birds: thank you, always.

ABOUT THE NATIONAL AUDUBON SOCIETY

 Audubon

The National Audubon Society protects birds and the places they need, today and tomorrow, throughout the Americas using science, advocacy, education, and on-the-ground conservation.

Audubon's state programs, nature centers, chapters, and partners have an unparalleled wingspan that reaches millions of people each year to inform, inspire, and unite diverse communities in conservation action.

Since 1905, Audubon's vision has been a world in which people and wildlife thrive. Audubon is a nonprofit conservation organization.

A Great Egret flies with nesting material—a true symbol of hope.

PHOTO CREDITS

Adam S. Frankel: Pages 26 (top), 60, 93

Ashok Khosla, seeingbirds.com: Pages 10, 14 (bottom right), 20 (top), 27 (top), 37 (top), 38 (top), 41 (top), 44, 45, 94

Bruce M. Beehler: Pages 40 (bottom), 76

Chris Willet: Pages 81 (all), 83 (bottom left and right)

Cindy Brown: Page 68

David Kinneer: Pages 7 (top), 13 (top), 14 (bottom left), 23 (left), 43, 67 (right), 87 (bottom)

F. Robert Wesley: Page 93 (left)

Fritz Waterman: Page 77 (top left)

George Radcliffe, Youth Maryland Ornithological Society leader: Page 52

Jana Burton Barker: Page 71

Jennifer Dudek: Page 14 (top left)

Kojo Baidoo: Page 6

Lily R. Smith: Page 51

Margaret A. Barker: Pages 53, 55 (right), 59, 65 (right), 67, 78, 79, 85 (top)

Matthew Addicks, Youth Maryland Ornithological Society: Pages 5 (top left and right), 15 (left middle), 16 (bottom left), 21 (top), 28 (top), 31 (top), 34 (top), 35 (top), 40 (top), 56, 65 (left)

Maxwell Ramey, Youth Maryland Ornithological Society: Pages 5 (bottom right), 36 (top)

Melanie Furr, Audubon Atlanta: Page 90

Melissa Groo: Page 88

Shutterstock: Pages 5 (top middle), 7 (bottom), 8, 19 (top), 22 (top), 25 (top), 32 (top), 42, 62, 74, 85 (bottom), 87 (top three in right column), 89

Steve Kress: Page 57, 63, 87 (top left)

Tookany/Tacony-Frankford Watershed Partnership, Inc.: Page 49 (bottom)

Vickie Henderson: Page 77 (illustrations)

Wil Hershberger, Nature Images and Sound, LLC: Pages 12 (top), 15 (top right), 16 (top right), 17 (top), 18 (top), 23 (right), 24 (top), 29 (top), 30 (top), 33 (top), 39 (top), 46, 49 (top), 73, 75

INDEX